SKINNY COOKIES, CAKES & SWEETS

Surrey Books

Chicago

SKINNY COOKIES, CAKES & SWEETS is published by Surrey Books, Inc., 230 E. Ohio St., Suite 120, Chicago, IL 60611.

First edition: 1 2 3 4 5

This book is manufactured in the United States of America.

Library of Congress Cataloging-in-Publication data:

Spitler, Sue.
    Skinny cookies, cakes & sweets / by Sue Spitler. — 1st ed.
        144   p.   cm.
    Includes index.
ISBN 0–940625–70–9 (pbk.): $12.95
    1. Reducing diet—Recipes. 2. Desserts. I. Title. II. Title:
Skinny cookies, cakes and sweets.
RM222.2.S684 1993
641.5'638–dc20   93–19876
                                                                        CIP

Editorial and production: *Bookcrafters, Inc., Chicago*
Nutritional analyses: *Linda R. Yoakum, M.S., R.D.*
Art direction: *Hughes & Co., Chicago*
Cover and interior illustrations by *Laurel DiGangi*

For free catalog and prices on quantity purchases, contact Surrey Books at the address above.

This title is distributed to the trade by Publishers Group West.

CONTENTS

Introduction v

1. CAKES 1
One dozen mouth-watering creations and old favorites.

2. PIES AND TARTS 21
5 scrumptious crusts and 11 delicious pies, from Sweet Potato
to Key Lime.

3. CHEESECAKES 39
Incredibly creamy and tempting, but all diet friendly.

4. COOKIES 45
Crinkles, squares, crisps, bars, brownies, macaroons,
biscotti—they're all here.

5. FRESH FRUIT DESSERTS 63
To your good health: 15 delightful low-cal treats, with so
little fat you can enjoy them every day.

6. FROZEN DESSERTS 79
9 tingling pleasures, including Sundaes, Tortoni, Sorbet, and
Baked Alaska.

7. CUSTARDS, PUDDINGS & SOUFFLES 89
Silky and luscious, from chocolate, bread, and rice puddings
to custards, flans, and 3 souffles.

8. DESSERT SAUCES 105
11 toppers from Raspberry Coulis and Brandied Berry to
Chocolate and Berries 'n Cream.

9. GOURMET ENDINGS 117
Yes! You *can* make Apricot and Peach Fillo Nests, Cassata
Siciliana, Custard Brûlée, and 8 more very elegant desserts.

Index 131

With Love . . .

to my grandmother, Ruth Buckley, who was a wonderful, dear friend and my most devoted cookie taster.

Acknowledgments

Many heartfelt thank you's to Cheryl Flynn, chef-associate, for her enthusiastic help in creating this cookbook. Cheryl tirelessly tested each recipe until it was flawless and helped calculate endless columns of fat and calorie figures. I'm also grateful to a good friend of long standing, Kathie German, and to a new friend, Joanne Leahy, for their helpful contributions in compiling mountains of copy and manuscript. My friends who volunteered for tasting are precious and too numerous to mention—thank you all!

INTRODUCTION

N ow it is possible to have your cake and eat it too—without those ominous pangs of guilt! In *Skinny Cookies, Cakes & Sweets,* we have proven that healthy desserts *can* taste utterly delicious—so delicious, in fact, that no one will know they're not laden with fat and calories—unless you tell them.

Traditionally, luscious cakes and desserts have been pleasurable to the palate but have not always been beneficial to our health. Research has proven that high-fat foods not only add calories and inches to the waistline but can contribute to heart, circulatory, and other health problems as well.

Skinny Cookies, Cakes & Sweets is filled with recipes that will appease any sweet tooth and gladden any occasion. You will find such traditional dessert favorites as Old-Fashioned Baked Rice Pudding, Streusel-Topped Carrot Cake, Key Lime Pie, Chewy Cocoa Brownies; ethnic delicacies such as Caramel Flan, Cassata Siciliana, Anise-Almond

Biscotti; and elegant offerings such as Apricot and Peach Fillo Nests, Herbed Custard Brulée, and Baked Fruit Compotes in Parchment.

Variety abounds, but *all* the recipes share one common element: they are low in fat, not exceeding the 30 percent of calories from fat guidelines recommended by the American Heart Association. Compare these figures to the fat ratios of most traditional desserts, which average 50 percent to 70 percent or even higher! When fat is reduced, so are calories. No dessert in this cookbook exceeds 250 calories per serving, and many are much less. Cookies average 50 calories or less, bar cookies 75 calories, and dessert sauces 40 calories or less per tablespoon.

Each recipe includes a nutritional analysis, detailing calories, fat, cholesterol, and sodium levels. Diabetic exchanges are also listed.

About 20 percent of the recipes can be made substituting artificial sweeteners for sugar. These recipes are designated by a large asterisk preceding their title. For equivalents, refer to the substitution directions stated on the specific sweetener you use. Remember that sweeteners with aspartame, such as Nutrasweet, cannot be used in baking and must be added to cooked foods after they have been removed from the heat, as prolonged exposure to oven or range heat will diminish sweetness.

So how were all of these healthful, tempting desserts created? Fortunately there are many wonderful new reduced-fat and non-fat ingredients available nationally in our supermarkets—yogurts, sour cream, cheeses. We substituted these new ingredients for their high-fat counterparts and incorporated other low-fat alternatives: skim or 2% milk for whole milk, cocoa for baking chocolate, egg whites for whole eggs or yolks, fresh fruit and purees for fat and oil. When a fat has been used, margarine has replaced butter. Although fresh eggs are listed in the recipes, those with special dietary requirements can use egg substitutes successfully.

Once armed with low-fat ingredients and many new ideas for using them, recipes were created, tested, and retested until they were deemed a delicious success. Chewy Cocoa Brownies were tested at least 12 times before unaware taste-testers came back for seconds and asked for the recipe. Cheesecakes were tested several times each, and crisp cookies (Cardamom Crisps, Chocolate-Glazed Cookie Crisps, Glazed Chocolate Shortbread Squares) had to be reformulated numerous times to finally achieve appropriate crispness. We were thrilled that pies and cakes were low enough in fat and calories to serve *real slices* rather than skimpy pieces. We marveled at the creaminess of the cheesecakes and the delicate, silky texture of the custards and puddings. Chocolate Fudge Meringues, Rich Chocolate Pudding, 3-layer sinful Chocolate Buttermilk Cake with Raspberry Cocoa Frosting, and other chocolate desserts were truly and honestly *chocolatey*. Streusel-Topped Carrot Cake was unbelievably moist. We could go on and on—but now it's time for *you* to head for the kitchen. *Bon appétit!*

1.
CAKES

◆

Streusel-Topped Carrot

Pumpkin Ginger

Banana Cinnamon

Chocolate-Cherry Pudding

Coffee-Frosted Cocoa

Chocolate Buttermilk Layer

Rich Lemon Pound

Orange Poppy Seed

Angel Food with Orange Sauce

Mocha Angel Food

Raspberry-Orange Swirl

Pineapple-Lemon Trifle

1

STREUSEL-TOPPED CARROT CAKE

The wonderful, rich carrot cakes we all love are usually laden with fat and calories. This version is every bit as delicious, moist, and rich—but unbelievably "skinny" on fat and calories.

12 Servings

Carrot Cake

- 1 cup packed light brown sugar
- 4 tablespoons margarine, softened
- 2 eggs
- 2 egg whites
- 3 cups carrots, shredded
- ½ cup dark raisins
- 2 cups all-purpose flour
- 1 teaspoon baking powder
- 1 teaspoon baking soda
- 1 teaspoon ground cinnamon
- ½ teaspoon ground nutmeg

Streusel Topping

- 3 tablespoons brown sugar
- 3 tablespoons all-purpose flour
- 1 tablespoon margarine

Carrot Cake: Preheat oven to 350°. Grease 9-inch springform pan lightly and sprinkle with flour.

Combine brown sugar and margarine in large bowl; beat until light and fluffy. Add eggs and egg whites, one at a time, beating well after each addition. Mix in carrots and raisins.

Combine flour, baking powder, baking soda, cinnamon, and nutmeg in medium-size bowl; add to batter. Mix well. Spoon batter into prepared pan.

Streusel Topping: Mix sugar and flour; cut in margarine until mixture resembles coarse crumbs. Sprinkle topping over batter.

Bake 30 to 35 minutes or until cake springs back when lightly touched in center. Cool in pan on wire rack 15 minutes; remove side from pan. Serve warm or at room temperature.

Nutritional Data

PER SERVING		EXCHANGES	
Calories:	231	Milk:	0.0
Fat (gm):	3.5	Veg.:	0.0
Cholesterol (mg):	35	Fruit:	0.0
Sodium (mg):	187	Bread:	3.0
Sat. fat (gm):	.7	Meat:	0.0
% Calories from fat:	13	Fat:	0.5

PUMPKIN GINGER CAKE

Moist and savory with spices, a perfect choice for fall and winter holidays. Serve with Tart Lemon or Warm Rum Sauce (see Index)!

8 Servings

½ cup canned pumpkin
½ cup packed light brown sugar
¼ cup margarine, softened
¼ cup light molasses
1 egg
1½ cups all-purpose flour
½ teaspoon baking powder
½ teaspoon baking soda
½ teaspoon ground allspice
½ teaspoon ground cloves
½ teaspoon ground ginger
Powdered sugar

Preheat oven to 350°. Grease 8-inch square baking dish lightly and sprinkle with flour.

Combine pumpkin, brown sugar, margarine, molasses, and egg in large mixer bowl; beat at medium speed until light and fluffy.

Combine flour, baking powder, baking soda, allspice, cloves, and ginger in medium bowl; add to pumpkin mixture. Blend at low speed until moistened. Pour batter into prepared pan.

Bake 30 to 35 minutes or until toothpick inserted in center comes out clean. Cool in pan on wire rack 10 minutes; remove from pan. Cool completely on wire rack. Dust lightly with powdered sugar before serving.

Nutritional Data

PER SERVING		EXCHANGES	
Calories:	201	Milk:	0.0
Fat (gm):	3.7	Veg.:	0.0
Cholesterol (mg):	27	Fruit:	0.0
Sodium (mg):	152	Bread:	2.5
Sat. fat (gm):	.7	Meat:	0.0
% Calories from fat:	17	Fat:	0.5

BANANA CINNAMON CAKE

Bananas add flavor and moistness to this picnic-perfect cake.

10 Servings

Cake

- 1½ cups all-purpose flour
- ½ cup packed light brown sugar
- 2 teaspoons baking powder
- 1 teaspoon baking soda
- 1 teaspoon ground cinnamon
- ¼ teaspoon salt
- 1 carton (6 ozs.) low-fat custard-style banana yogurt
- 1 cup ripe banana, mashed (1 medium banana)
- 2 tablespoons margarine, softened
- 2 egg whites
- 1 teaspoon vanilla

Powdered Sugar Frosting

- 1 cup powdered sugar
- 2 tablespoons margarine, melted
- 2 tablespoons skim milk

Cake: Preheat oven to 375°. Grease 9-inch-square baking pan lightly; sprinkle with flour.

Combine flour, sugar, baking powder, baking soda, cinnamon, and salt in large bowl.

Mix yogurt, banana, margarine, egg whites, and vanilla in medium bowl; stir into flour mixture and mix well. Pour batter into prepared pan.

Bake 25 to 30 minutes or until cake springs back when lightly touched in center. Cool in pan on wire rack 10 minutes; invert onto wire rack and cool completely.

Powdered Sugar Frosting: Combine powdered sugar, margarine, and milk in small bowl; beat until smooth. Spread frosting over cooled cake.

Nutritional Data

PER SERVING		EXCHANGES	
Calories:	198	Milk:	0.0
Fat (gm):	2.8	Veg.:	0.0
Cholesterol (mg):	1	Fruit:	0.0
Sodium (mg):	278	Bread:	2.5
Sat. fat (gm):	.4	Meat:	0.0
% Calories from fat:	13	Fat:	0.5

CHOCOLATE-CHERRY PUDDING CAKE

Served warm, this fudgey favorite will bring smiles to kids of all ages.

14 Servings

1¾ cups all-purpose flour
1¼ cups granulated sugar
⅓ cup unsweetened cocoa
3 tablespoons baking powder
¾ cup skim milk
½ cup unsweetened applesauce
1 cup fresh or frozen sweet cherries, thawed and pitted
¼ cup chopped pecans
1¼ cups packed dark brown sugar
3 cups hot water
¼ cup unsweetened cocoa

P reheat oven to 350°. Grease 9×13-inch baking pan lightly.

Combine flour, granulated sugar, ⅓ cup cocoa, and baking powder in large bowl; stir in milk and applesauce just until dry ingredients are moistened. Fold in cherries and pecans; spoon batter into prepared pan.

Combine brown sugar, hot water, and ¼ cup cocoa in medium bowl, stirring until smooth. Pour brown sugar mixture over batter.

Bake 35 to 40 minutes or until set (cake will have a pudding-like texture). Serve warm or at room temperature.

Nutritional Data

PER SERVING		EXCHANGES	
Calories:	242	Milk:	0.0
Fat (gm):	1.9	Veg.:	0.0
Cholesterol (mg):	0	Fruit:	1.5
Sodium (mg):	264	Bread:	2.0
Sat. fat (gm):	.2	Meat:	0.0
% Calories from fat:	7	Fat:	0.0

COFFEE-FROSTED COCOA CAKE

For company fare, make this cake in a 9-inch springform pan (bake 40 to 45 minutes). Add enough milk to the frosting to make a glaze consistency; spread glaze over top of cake, allowing it to drizzle down the side.

16 Servings

Cake

- 1½ cups sugar
- ½ cup margarine, softened
- 2 eggs
- 1 teaspoon vanilla
- 2 cups all-purpose flour
- ¾ cup unsweetened cocoa
- 2 teaspoons baking soda
- 1 teaspoon salt
- 1 cup skim milk

Coffee Frosting

- 1 tablespoon instant coffee granules
- 1 tablespoon hot water
- 1 tablespoon margarine, softened
- 1 cup powdered sugar
- 2-3 tablespoons skim milk

Cake: Preheat oven to 350°. Grease 13×9-inch pan lightly and sprinkle with flour.

Combine sugar and margarine in large bowl; beat until light and fluffy. Add eggs one at a time, beating well after each addition. Stir in vanilla.

Combine flour, cocoa, baking soda, and salt in medium bowl. Mix dry ingredients into egg mixture alternately with milk, blending well.

Bake 25 to 35 minutes or until toothpick inserted in center comes out clean and cake begins to pull away from sides of pan. Cool completely on wire rack.

Coffee Frosting: Dissolve coffee in hot water in medium bowl. Beat in margarine, powdered sugar, and enough milk for spreading consistency. Spread Coffee Frosting over cooled cake.

Nutritional Data

PER SERVING		EXCHANGES	
Calories:	203	Milk:	0.0
Fat (gm):	4.5	Veg.:	0.0
Cholesterol (mg):	27	Fruit:	0.0
Sodium (mg):	327	Bread:	2.5
Sat. fat (gm):	.8	Meat:	0.0
% Calories from fat:	20	Fat:	0.5

CHOCOLATE BUTTERMILK LAYER CAKE WITH RASPBERRY COCOA FROSTING

This "skinny" cake is an unbelievable 3 layers high, generously iced with raspberry-spiked frosting.

16 Servings

Cake
- 2 cups cake flour
- ½ cup unsweetened cocoa
- 2 teaspoons baking powder
- ½ teaspoon baking soda
- 1 teaspoon salt
- 1½ cups sugar
- 4 tablespoons margarine, softened
- 2 eggs
- 2 egg whites
- 1 teaspoon vanilla
- 1 cup buttermilk

Raspberry Cocoa Frosting
- 3-4 tablespoons unsweetened cocoa
- 2 tablespoons raspberry-flavor liqueur
- 3 cups powdered sugar
- 3-4 tablespoons skim milk
- Powdered sugar (optional)
- Fresh raspberries (optional)

Cake: Preheat oven to 350°. Lightly grease three 8-inch round cake pans and sprinkle with flour. Line bottoms of pans with waxed paper.

Combine flour, cocoa, baking powder, baking soda, and salt in medium bowl; set aside.

Combine sugar and margarine in large bowl; beat until light and fluffy. Add eggs and egg whites one at a time, beating well after each addition. Stir in vanilla. Mix in flour mixture alternately with buttermilk, beginning and ending with flour, blending well.

Divide batter evenly among prepared pans. Bake 25 to 30 minutes or until toothpicks inserted in centers come out clean. Cool in pans on wire racks 10 minutes; remove from pans. Cool completely on wire racks.

Raspberry Cocoa Frosting: Combine cocoa and liqueur in small bowl until smooth. Stir in powdered sugar and enough milk for spreading consistency.

Place one cake layer, top side down, on serving plate; spread evenly with about ⅓ of frosting. Top with second cake layer and ⅓ frosting; repeat with remaining cake layer and frosting. Garnish with powdered sugar and fresh raspberries, if desired.

Note: Rounded tops of cakes can be trimmed to make assembling and frosting easier.

Nutritional Data

PER SERVING		EXCHANGES	
Calories:	236	Milk:	0.0
Fat (gm):	2.8	Veg.:	0.0
Cholesterol (mg):	27	Fruit:	0.0
Sodium (mg):	266	Bread:	3.0
Sat. fat (gm):	.5	Meat:	0.0
% Calories from fat:	10	Fat:	0.5

Rich Lemon Pound Cake

Savor the richness of this cake—serve each slice with a tablespoon of Orange Marmalade Sauce (see Index) for an added citrus accent.

12 Servings

Cake

¾ cup sugar
⅓ cup margarine, softened
1 cup low-fat sour cream
3 egg whites
2 teaspoons lemon juice
1 tablespoon lemon rind, grated
2½ cups cake flour
1 teaspoon baking soda
¼ teaspoon salt

Lemon Syrup

⅔ cup powdered sugar
¼ cup lemon juice
3 tablespoons water
Powdered sugar

Cake: Preheat oven to 350°. Grease 6-cup fluted cake pan lightly and sprinkle with flour.

In large bowl, beat sugar and margarine until smooth and fluffy. Beat in sour cream, egg whites, lemon juice, and lemon rind until smooth.

Combine flour, baking soda, and salt in small bowl and add to batter. Beat until smooth, about 1 minute.

Spoon batter into prepared pan and bake 40 to 50 minutes or until toothpick inserted in center comes out clean. Cool in pan on wire rack 20 minutes; invert onto wire rack. Meanwhile, make syrup.

Lemon Syrup: Combine sugar, lemon juice, and water in small saucepan. Heat to boiling, stirring constantly until sugar is dissolved. Cool slightly.

With a skewer or tines of fork, pierce cake top at 1-inch intervals. Spoon warm syrup over cake; sprinkle with powdered sugar.

Nutritional Data

PER SERVING		EXCHANGES	
Calories:	230	Milk:	0.0
Fat (gm):	6	Veg.:	0.0
Cholesterol (mg):	0	Fruit:	0.0
Sodium (mg):	205	Bread:	2.5
Sat. fat (gm):	3.1	Meat:	0.0
% Calories from fat:	23	Fat:	1.0

ORANGE POPPY SEED CAKE

This citrus-fresh cake is a perfect addition to any brunch menu.

12 Servings

Cake

- ½ cup sugar
- 6 tablespoons margarine, softened
- 2 egg whites
- 1 egg
- ¾ cup reduced-fat sour cream
- 2 tablespoons frozen orange juice concentrate, thawed
- 2 cups cake flour
- 2 tablespoons poppy seeds
- 1 teaspoon baking powder
- ½ teaspoon baking soda
- ¼ teaspoon salt

Orange Glaze

- 1 cup powdered sugar
- 3-4 tablespoons orange juice

Cake: Preheat oven to 350°. Grease 6-cup fluted cake pan lightly and sprinkle with flour.

In large bowl, beat sugar and margarine until smooth and fluffy. Beat in egg whites, egg, sour cream, and orange juice until smooth.

Combine cake flour, poppy seeds, baking powder, baking soda, and salt in medium bowl; add to sour cream batter. Beat on medium-high speed until smooth, about 1 to 2 minutes. Pour batter into prepared pan.

Bake 40 to 55 minutes or until toothpick inserted in center comes out clean. Cool in pan on wire rack 25 to 30 minutes; invert onto wire rack.

Orange Glaze: Combine sugar and enough orange juice to make glaze consistency. Drizzle cake with Orange Glaze.

Nutritional Data

PER SERVING		EXCHANGES	
Calories:	201	Milk:	0.0
Fat (gm):	6.5	Veg.:	0.0
Cholesterol (mg):	18	Fruit:	0.0
Sodium (mg):	201	Bread:	2.0
Sat. fat (gm):	2.7	Meat:	0.0
% Calories from fat:	29	Fat:	1.0

ANGEL FOOD CAKE WITH ORANGE SAUCE

For flavor accent, toast cake slices lightly under the broiler and add small scoops of low-fat frozen vanilla yogurt before topping with sauce.

8 Servings

- 1 pkg. (6.95 ozs.) angel food loaf cake mix
- ½ cup water
- ½ cup hazelnuts or almonds, coarsely chopped, toasted
- 1 cup orange juice
- 2 tablespoons orange-flavor liqueur
- 2 medium oranges, peeled and sectioned

Preheat oven to 375°.

Combine cake mix and water in large bowl. Mix at low speed until moistened. Beat 2 minutes at high speed. Fold in nuts and pour into ungreased 9×5-inch loaf pan. Bake 25 to 30 minutes or until cracks on top appear dry. Cool completely in pan, tipped on side on wire rack.

Combine orange juice and liqueur in small saucepan. Heat to boiling, reduce heat, and simmer 10 minutes. Add oranges and simmer until heated through; spoon over cake slices.

Nutritional Data

PER SERVING		EXCHANGES	
Calories:	185	Milk:	0.0
Fat (gm):	4.6	Veg.:	0.0
Cholesterol (mg):	0	Fruit:	0.5
Sodium (mg):	196	Bread:	1.5
Sat. fat (gm):	.3	Meat:	0.0
% Calories from fat:	22	Fat:	1.0

MOCHA ANGEL FOOD CAKE WITH BITTERSWEET CHOCOLATE SAUCE

If chocolate is good, it's even better with angel food!

12 Servings

1 package (16 ozs.) angel food cake mix
1⅓ cups cold water
3 tablespoons unsweetened cocoa
2 tablespoons instant espresso coffee granules
1½ cups Bittersweet Chocolate Sauce (see Index)

Preheat oven to 350°.

Mix cake mix, water, cocoa, and espresso in large mixer bowl; beat at low speed until moistened. Beat a high speed until stiff peaks form, about 2 minutes. Pour batter into ungreased 12-cup tube pan.

Bake 45 to 48 minutes or until cracks on top appear dry. Invert cake in pan onto funnel or glass bottle; cool completely. Remove cake from pan and serve with Chocolate Sauce.

Nutritional Data

PER SERVING		EXCHANGES	
Calories:	210	Milk:	0.0
Fat (gm):	1.8	Veg.:	0.0
Cholesterol (mg):	0	Fruit:	0.0
Sodium (mg):	331	Bread:	3.0
Sat. fat (gm):	.2	Meat:	0.0
% Calories from fat:	8	Fat:	0.0

RASPBERRY-ORANGE SWIRL CAKE

A swirl of raspberry puree enhances flavor and appearance in this delectable cake.

14 Servings

2 cups fresh or frozen and thawed raspberries
1 pkg. (18.5 ozs.) reduced-fat yellow cake mix
1 cup water
2 tablespoons frozen orange juice concentrate, thawed
3 egg whites
½ teaspoon orange extract
2 teaspoons orange rind, grated
2 cups powdered sugar
½ teaspoon orange extract
3-4 tablespoons skim milk

P reheat oven to 350°. Grease 12-cup fluted cake pan lightly and sprinkle with flour.

Process raspberries in food processor or blender until smooth; strain and discard seeds.

Combine cake mix, water, orange juice, egg whites, and ½ teaspoon orange extract in mixer bowl. Beat on medium-high speed until smooth, about 2 minutes; stir in orange rind.

Pour half the batter into prepared pan; spoon on raspberry puree and top with remaining batter. With a knife, cut through batter a few times to marbleize.

Bake 40 to 45 minutes or until toothpick inserted in center comes out clean. Cool in pan on wire rack 20 minutes; remove from pan. Cool completely on wire rack.

Combine powdered sugar and ½ teaspoon orange extract in small bowl; stir in enough milk to make glaze consistency. Spoon over cake.

Nutritional Data

PER SERVING		EXCHANGES	
Calories:	229	Milk:	0.0
Fat (gm):	2.7	Veg.:	0.0
Cholesterol (mg):	0	Fruit:	1.0
Sodium (mg):	266	Bread:	2.0
Sat. fat (gm):	.9	Meat:	0.0
% Calories from fat:	11	Fat:	0.5

PINEAPPLE-LEMON TRIFLE

Select your prettiest glass bowl for serving this attractive dessert. A fruit puree replaces the more traditional preserves, enhancing the use of fresh fruits in this recipe.

12 Servings

1 pkg. (18.25 ozs.) reduced-fat white cake mix
1⅓ cups water
3 egg whites
1½ cups pineapple chunks in juice, drained
    Lemon Custard (recipe follows)
1 pt. strawberries, sliced
2 medium bananas, sliced
¾ cup frozen light whipped topping, thawed

Preheat oven to 350°.

Prepare cake mix according to package directions, using 1⅓ cups water and 3 egg whites. Bake in lightly greased and floured 13×9-inch baking pan 28 to 30 minutes or until top springs back when touched. Cool on wire rack. Cut half the cake into 1-inch cubes. (Reserve or freeze remaining cake for another use.)

Process pineapple chunks in blender or food processor until smooth. Layer ⅓ of cake cubes in bottom of 2-quart glass serving bowl. Spoon ⅓ Lemon Custard and ⅓ pineapple puree over cake cubes; top with ⅓ of the strawberries and bananas. Repeat layers twice. Refrigerate until chilled, about 1 hour. Garnish with whipped topping.

Lemon Custard

¼ cup sugar
2 tablespoons cornstarch
2 tablespoons flour
1 cup skim milk
⅓ cup lemon juice
2 eggs, slightly beaten
¼ teaspoon ground nutmeg

Mix sugar, cornstarch, and flour in medium saucepan; stir in milk and lemon juice. Cook over medium heat until mixture boils and thickens; boil 1 minute, stirring constantly.

Stir about ½ cup of mixture into eggs; stir egg mixture back into saucepan. Cook over low heat, stirring constantly, until thickened. Remove from heat; stir in nutmeg. Refrigerate until chilled, 1 to 2 hours.

Nutritional Data

PER SERVING		EXCHANGES	
Calories:	191	Milk:	0.0
Fat (gm):	3.6	Veg.:	0.0
Cholesterol (mg):	36	Fruit:	1.0
Sodium (mg):	192	Bread:	1.5
Sat. fat (gm):	.8	Meat:	0.0
% Calories from fat:	16	Fat:	0.5

2.
PIES AND TARTS

Basic Pie Crusts

Meringue Pie Crust

Graham Cracker Crumb Crust

Vanilla Crumb Crust

Gingersnap Crumb Crust

Old-Fashioned Buttermilk Pie

Spiced Sweet Potato Pie

Banana-Strawberry Cream Pie

Toasted Coconut Cream Tart

Chocolate Rum Pie

Key Lime Pie

Kiwi Tart

Lemon Cloud Pie

Tarte Tatin

Raspberry-Glazed Blueberry Tart

Pear Tart with Crème Anglaise

*Basic Pie Crust (All-Purpose Flour)

This pastry contains a minimum of margarine yet is not difficult to handle or roll. Use cold margarine and ice water, as the recipe directs.

8 Servings

1¼ cups all-purpose flour
2 tablespoons sugar (substitute can be used, but not aspartame*)
¼ teaspoon salt
3 tablespoons cold margarine
4-5 tablespoons ice water

C ombine flour, sugar,* and salt in medium bowl. With pastry blender or 2 knives, cut in margarine until mixture resembles coarse crumbs. Sprinkle with water, 1 tablespoon at a time, mixing lightly with a fork after each addition until pastry just holds together.

On lightly floured surface, roll dough into a circle 2 inches larger in diameter than pie pan. Wrap pastry around rolling pin and unroll into 8- or 9-inch pie or tart pan, easing it into bottom and side of pan. Trim edges, fold under, and flute. Bake as pie recipe directs.

Makes one 8- or 9-inch pie crust.

Note: When a pie crust is baked before it is filled, the recipe will indicate baking with weights so that bottom of crust remains flat. Line bottom of pastry with aluminum foil and fill with a single layer of pie weights or dried beans. Remove weights and foil 5 minutes before end of baking time indicated in recipe. If not using weights or dried beans, piercing the bottom of the pastry with the tines of a fork will help crust remain flat.

Nutritional Data

PER SERVING			EXCHANGES	
Calories:	101	(91)	Milk:	0.0
Fat (gm):	2.3		Veg.:	0.0
Cholesterol (mg):	0		Fruit:	0.0
Sodium (mg):	116	(117)	Bread:	1.0
Sat. fat (gm):	.4		Meat:	0.0
% Calories from fat:	21	(23)	Fat:	0.5

(*Changes shown in parentheses will result from substituting Sweet 'n Low® for sugar.)

*Basic Pie Crust (Cake Flour)

This pastry also contains a minimum of margarine but uses cake flour, which is lower in calories than all-purpose flour.

8 Servings

- 1¼ cups cake flour
- 1 tablespoon sugar (substitute can be used, but not aspartame*)
- ¼ teaspoon salt
- 3 tablespoons cold margarine
- 3-4 tablespoons ice water

C ombine cake flour, sugar,* and salt in medium bowl. With pastry blender or 2 knives, cut in margarine until mixture resembles coarse crumbs. Sprinkle in water, 1 tablespoon at a time, mixing lightly with a fork after each addition until pastry just holds together.

On lightly floured surface, roll dough into a circle 2 inches larger in diameter than pie pan. Wrap pastry around rolling pin and unroll into 8- or 9-inch pie or tart pan, easing it into bottom and side of pan. Trim edges, fold under, and flute. Bake as pie recipe directs.

Makes one 8-inch pie crust.

Note: When a pie crust is baked before it is filled, the recipe will indicate baking with weights so that bottom of crust remains flat. Line bottom of pastry with aluminum foil and fill with a single layer of pie weights or dried beans. Remove weights and foil 5 minutes before end of baking time indicated in recipe. If not using weights or dried beans, piercing the bottom of the pastry with the tines of a fork will help crust remain flat.

Nutritional Data

PER SERVING			EXCHANGES	
Calories:	86	(81)	Milk:	0.0
Fat (gm):	2.3		Veg.:	0.0
Cholesterol (mg):	0		Fruit:	0.0
Sodium (mg):	49	(50)	Bread:	1.0
Sat. fat (gm):	.4		Meat:	0.0
% Calories from fat:	24	(26)	Fat:	0.5

(*Changes shown in parentheses will result from substituting Sweet 'n Low® for sugar.)

MERINGUE PIE CRUST

Light, airy, delicious, and versatile. Fill this crust with scoops of low-fat frozen yogurt and top with a light drizzle of Warm Rum or Bittersweet Chocolate Sauce (see Index).

8 Servings

4 egg whites
⅛ teaspoon cream of tartar
1 cup sugar

Preheat oven to 350°.

Beat egg whites and cream of tartar in medium bowl to soft peaks. Gradually beat in sugar, beating to stiff peaks. Spoon mixture into ungreased 8- or 9-inch glass pie pan, spreading on bottom and up side to form a large bowl shape. Bake 40 minutes or until firm to touch and lightly browned. Cool on wire rack.

Makes one 8- or 9-inch crust.

Nutritional Data

PER SERVING		EXCHANGES	
Calories:	98	Milk:	0.0
Fat (gm):	0	Veg.:	0.0
Cholesterol (mg):	0	Fruit:	1.0
Sodium (mg):	28	Bread:	0.0
Sat. fat (gm):	0	Meat:	0.5
% Calories from fat:	0	Fat:	0.0

GRAHAM CRACKER CRUMB CRUST

Mix this crust right in the pie pan—quick and easy!

8 Servings

1¼ cups graham cracker crumbs
2 tablespoons sugar
3 tablespoons margarine, melted

H eat oven to 350°. Combine graham crumbs, sugar, and margarine in 8- or 9-inch pie pan; pat mixture evenly on bottom and side of pan. Bake 8 to 10 minutes or until edge is lightly browned. Cool on wire rack.
Makes one 8- or 9-inch pie crust.

Nutritional Data

PER SERVING		EXCHANGES	
Calories:	91	Milk:	0.0
Fat (gm):	3.2	Veg.:	0.0
Cholesterol (mg):	0	Fruit:	0.0
Sodium (mg):	122	Bread:	1.0
Sat. fat (gm):	.6	Meat:	0.0
% Calories from fat:	32*	Fat:	0.5

*Percentage of calories from fat will decrease in servings of actual pie.

VANILLA CRUMB CRUST

A perfect recipe when a delicately flavored crust is desired.

8 Servings

1 cup vanilla wafer cookie crumbs
2 tablespoons margarine, melted

Heat oven to 350°. Combine vanilla crumbs and margarine in 8- or 9-inch pie pan; pat mixture evenly on bottom and side of pan. Bake 8 to 10 minutes or until edge is lightly browned. Cool on wire rack. Makes one 8- or 9-inch pie crust.

Nutritional Data

PER SERVING		EXCHANGES	
Calories:	70	Milk:	0.0
Fat (gm):	3.3	Veg.:	0.0
Cholesterol (mg):	8	Fruit:	0.0
Sodium (mg):	64	Bread:	0.5
Sat. fat (gm):	.6	Meat:	0.0
% Calories from fat:	43*	Fat:	0.5

(*Percentage of calories from fat will decrease in servings of actual pie.)

GINGERSNAP CRUMB CRUST

Gingersnaps provide a zesty flavor accent in this crust.

8 Servings

½ cup graham cracker crumbs
½ cup gingersnap cookie crumbs
2 tablespoons margarine

Heat oven to 350°. Combine graham crumbs, gingersnap crumbs, and margarine in 8- or 9-inch pie pan; pat mixture evenly on bottom and side of pan. Bake 8 to 10 minutes or until edge is lightly browned. Cool on wire rack.

Makes one 8- or 9-inch pie crust.

Nutritional Data

PER SERVING		EXCHANGES	
Calories:	68	Milk:	0.0
Fat (gm):	3.3	Veg.:	0.0
Cholesterol (mg):	0	Fruit:	0.0
Sodium (mg):	79	Bread:	0.5
Sat. fat (gm):	.3	Meat:	0.0
% Calories from fat:	44*	Fat:	0.5

(*Percentage of calories from fat will decrease in servings of actual pie.)

OLD-FASHIONED BUTTERMILK PIE

Carry on grandma's best traditions with this pie!

8 Servings

Gingersnap Crumb Crust (see preceding recipe)
¾ cup sugar
2 tablespoons margarine, softened
1 egg
2 egg whites
3 tablespoons flour
¼ teaspoon salt
1 cup buttermilk
Ground nutmeg

Make pie crust, using 8-inch pie pan. Preheat oven to 300°.

Mix sugar and margarine in medium bowl until blended; beat in egg and egg whites. Stir in flour, salt, and buttermilk until well blended.

Pour filling into prepared crust; bake 40 minutes or until sharp knife inserted near center comes out clean. Sprinkle with nutmeg and serve warm or chilled.

Nutritional Data

PER SERVING		EXCHANGES	
Calories:	184	Milk:	0.0
Fat (gm):	5.7	Veg.:	0.0
Cholesterol (mg):	28	Fruit:	0.0
Sodium (mg):	233	Bread:	2.0
Sat. fat (gm):	1	Meat:	0.0
% Calories from fat:	27	Fat:	1.0

*SPICED SWEET POTATO PIE

A change from traditional pumpkin, this pie will brighten any winter holiday table.

10 Servings

Basic Pie Crust (All-Purpose Flour, see Index)
1½ cups sweet potatoes, peeled, cooked, and mashed
¾ cup packed light brown sugar (substitute can be used, but not aspartame*)
1 egg
2 egg whites
1½ cups skim milk
1 teaspoon ground cinnamon
1 teaspoon ground ginger
½ teaspoon ground mace
¼ teaspoon salt
Frozen light whipped topping, thawed (optional)

P reheat oven to 350°. Prepare pie crust, using 8-inch pie pan.
Pierce bottom of pastry with fork, and bake without weights 10 minutes or until very light brown. Cool on wire rack.

Beat sweet potatoes, brown sugar,* egg, and egg whites in medium bowl until smooth. Mix in milk, cinnamon, ginger, mace, and salt. Pour into pie crust.

Bake about 45 minutes or until sharp knife inserted near center comes out clean. Serve warm or at room temperature; garnish with whipped topping.

Nutritional Data

PER SERVING			EXCHANGES	
Calories:	218	(156)	Milk:	0.0
Fat (gm):	2.5		Veg.:	0.0
Cholesterol (mg):	22		Fruit:	0.0
Sodium (mg):	140	(143)	Bread:	2.5 (2.0)
Sat. fat (gm):	.6		Meat:	0.0
% Calories from fat:	11	(15)	Fat:	0.5

(*Changes shown in parentheses will result from substituting 21 packets Sweet 'n Low® for brown sugar.)

BANANA-STRAWBERRY CREAM PIE

Strawberries add a new twist to this old favorite. Refrigerate until the cream filling is set and well chilled before slicing.

8 Servings

Graham Cracker Crumb Crust (see Index)
¼ cup graham cracker crumbs
1 tablespoon margarine
⅓ cup sugar
¼ cup cornstarch
2 tablespoons flour
⅛ teaspoon salt
2½ cups skim milk
3 egg yolks
1 teaspoon vanilla
¼ teaspoon ground cinnamon
⅛ teaspoon ground nutmeg
1 cup sliced strawberries
2 medium bananas

Make pie crust, adding ¼ cup graham crumbs and 1 tablespoon margarine to recipe and using 9-inch pie pan.

Mix sugar, cornstarch, flour, and salt in medium saucepan; stir in milk. Cook over medium heat until mixture boils and thickens; boil 1 minute, stirring constantly.

Stir about ½ cup of mixture into egg yolks; stir egg mixture back into saucepan. Cook over low heat, stirring constantly, until thickened.

Remove from heat; stir in vanilla, cinnamon, and nutmeg. Cool to room temperature, stirring frequently. Refrigerate until chilled, 1 to 2 hours.

Set aside 4 to 6 strawberry slices. Slice 1 to 1½ bananas and arrange in crust with remaining strawberries. Spoon custard into crust; refrigerate until set, 4 to 6 hours. Slice remaining banana and garnish pie with banana and strawberry slices.

Nutritional Data

PER SERVING		EXCHANGES	
Calories:	234	Milk:	1.0
Fat (gm):	6.4	Veg.:	0.0
Cholesterol (mg):	81	Fruit:	0.0
Sodium (mg):	212	Bread:	1.5
Sat. fat (gm):	1.4	Meat:	0.0
% Calories from fat:	24	Fat:	1.0

*TOASTED COCONUT CREAM TART

Tucked in a tart pan for a new look, you'll enjoy this updated version of an old favorite.

---

8 Servings

Basic Pie Crust (Cake Flour, see Index)
⅓ cup sugar (substitute can be used*)
2 tablespoons cornstarch
1½ cups 2% milk
1 egg, slightly beaten
¼ cup toasted, unsweetened, flaked coconut

| P |

reheat oven to 375°. Prepare pie crust, using 9-inch tart pan.
Line pastry with weights, and bake 10 to 15 minutes or until lightly browned. Cool on wire rack.

Mix sugar* and cornstarch in small saucepan; stir in milk. Cook over medium heat until mixture boils and thickens; boil 1 minute, stirring constantly.

Stir about ½ cup of mixture into egg; stir egg mixture back into saucepan. Cook over low heat, stirring constantly, until thickened. Stir in 3 tablespoons of coconut.

Pour custard into cooled pie crust, spreading evenly. Sprinkle with remaining 1 tablespoon coconut. Cool to room temperature. Refrigerate until set, 2 to 4 hours.

Note: If using sweeteners with aspartame, stir into filling after it has been cooked and cooled slightly.

Nutritional Data

PER SERVING			EXCHANGES		
Calories:	170	(139)	Milk:	0.0	
Fat (gm):	4.9		Veg.:	0.0	
Cholesterol (mg):	30		Fruit:	0.0	
Sodium (mg):	85		Bread:	2.0	(1.5)
Sat. fat (gm):	1.1		Meat:	0.0	
% Calories from fat:	26	(30)	Fat:	1.0	

(*Changes shown in parentheses will result from substituting 8 packets Equal® for sugar.)

CHOCOLATE RUM PIE

Dutch or European process cocoa gives a special rich chocolate flavor to the filling in this delicious pie.

8 Servings

Vanilla Crumb Crust (see Index)
1 envelope unflavored gelatin
½ cup 2% milk
½ cup sugar
2 tablespoons dark rum
½ cup Dutch process (unsweetened) cocoa
1 teaspoon rum extract
1 envelope (1.3 ozs.) whipped topping (such as Dream Whip)
½ cup 2% milk

Make pie crust, using 8-inch pie pan.

Sprinkle gelatin over ½ cup milk in small saucepan; let stand 2 to 3 minutes. Stir in sugar and rum. Cook over low heat, stirring constantly, until gelatin and sugar are dissolved. Remove from heat, stir in cocoa and rum extract.

When gelatin mixture is partially set (consistency of unbeaten egg whites), blend whipped topping and ½ cup milk in deep bowl; beat at high speed until topping forms soft peaks, about 4 minutes. Fold topping into gelatin mixture. Spoon mixture into cooled pie crust; refrigerate until set, about 2 to 4 hours.

Nutritional Data

PER SERVING		EXCHANGES	
Calories:	170	Milk:	0.0
Fat (gm):	5.7	Veg.:	0.0
Cholesterol (mg):	10	Fruit:	0.0
Sodium (mg):	83	Bread:	2.0
Sat. fat (gm):	.9	Meat:	0.0
% Calories from fat:	30	Fat:	0.5

*KEY LIME PIE

Use key lime juice in this pie, if available, for the best flavor.

8 Servings

Basic Pie Crust (Cake Flour, see Index)
¾ cup sugar (substitute can be used*)
1 envelope unflavored gelatin
1¼ cups skim milk
6 ozs. reduced-fat cream cheese, softened**
⅓-½ cup fresh lime juice
Lime slices
Fresh mint

P reheat oven to 350°. Prepare pie crust, using 8-inch pie pan.
Line pastry with weights, and bake until golden brown, 15 to 20 minutes. Cool on wire rack.

Mix sugar* and gelatin in small saucepan; stir in milk. Cook over low heat until sugar and gelatin are dissolved, stirring constantly; remove from heat.

Beat cream cheese in small bowl until fluffy; beat in lime juice until smooth. Gradually add milk mixture, mixing until smooth.

Pour into cooled pie crust. Refrigerate until set, about 2 to 4 hours. Garnish with lime slices and mint.

*Note: If using sweeteners with aspartame, stir into filling after it has been cooked and cooled slightly.

**Note: If using artificial sweetener, substitute non-fat cream cheese.

Nutritional Data

PER SERVING			EXCHANGES	
Calories:	222	(117)	Milk:	0.5
Fat (gm):	7.3	(2.3)	Veg.:	0.0
Cholesterol (mg):	17	(4)	Fruit:	0.0
Sodium (mg):	155	(197)	Bread:	2.0 (1.0)
Sat. fat (gm):	3.5	(.4)	Meat:	0.0
% Calories from fat:	29	(19)	Fat:	1.0 (0.0)

(*Changes shown in parentheses will result from substituting Equal®
and non-fat cream cheese.)

*KIWI TART

Add other sliced spring or summer fruit to this tart if you wish.

8 Servings

Basic Pie Crust (Cake Flour, see Index)
¼ cup sugar (substitute can be used*)
2 tablespoons cornstarch
1¼ cups 2% milk
1 tablespoon lemon juice
1 egg, slightly beaten
½ lb. kiwi fruit (5 medium), peeled and sliced

Preheat oven to 375°. Prepare pie crust, using 9-inch tart pan. Line pastry with weights, and bake 10 to 15 minutes or until lightly browned. Cool on wire rack.

Mix sugar* and cornstarch in small saucepan; stir in milk and lemon juice. Cook over medium heat until mixture boils and thickens; boil 1 minute, stirring constantly.

Stir about ½ cup milk mixture into egg; stir egg mixture back into saucepan. Cook over low heat, stirring constantly, until thickened.

Spoon hot custard into cooled pie crust, spreading evenly; cool to room temperature. Lightly cover custard with plastic wrap; refrigerate 2 to 4 hours or until set. Just before serving, arrange kiwi slices in overlapping circles on custard.

*Note: If you use a sweetener with aspartame in the custard filling, add after custard has been cooked and cooled several minutes.

Nutritional Data

PER SERVING			EXCHANGES	
Calories:	168	(139)	Milk:	0.0
Fat (gm):	3.8		Veg.:	0.0
Cholesterol (mg):	29		Fruit:	1.0 (0.5)
Sodium (mg):	78		Bread:	1.0
Sat. fat (gm):	1		Meat:	0.0
% Calories from fat:	20	(24)	Fat:	1.0

(*Changes shown in parentheses will result from substituting 9 packets Equal® for sugar.)

LEMON CLOUD PIE

Other flavors of this wonderful dessert are easy. Just substitute another low-fat fruit yogurt for the lemon—strawberry, raspberry, or cherry are possible choices.

8 Servings

Meringue Pie Crust (see Index)
1½ cups frozen light whipped non-dairy topping, thawed
1½ cups low-fat custard-style lemon yogurt
2 tablespoons lemon rind, grated
Lemon slices

Make pie crust, using 9-inch pie pan. Combine whipped topping, yogurt, and lemon rind in small bowl. Spoon into center of meringue shell. Garnish with lemon slices.

Nutritional Data

PER SERVING		EXCHANGES	
Calories:	170	Milk:	0.5
Fat (gm):	3.5	Veg.:	0.0
Cholesterol (mg):	2	Fruit:	2.0
Sodium (mg):	62	Bread:	0.0
Sat. fat (gm):	.3	Meat:	0.0
% Calories from fat:	17	Fat:	0.5

TARTE TATIN

Caramelized sugar contributes special flavor to this French-style upside-down apple tart.

8 Servings

- 1 cup cake flour
- 2 tablespoons sugar
- 3 tablespoons cold margarine
- 2-3 tablespoons ice water
- 5 cups Granny Smith apples (about 2 ½ lbs.), peeled, cored, and cut into scant ½-inch slices
- ½ cup sugar
- ¼ teaspoon ground nutmeg
- 1 tablespoon lemon juice
- ¼ cup sugar
- 2 tablespoons margarine

C ombine cake flour and sugar in medium bowl. With pastry blender or 2 knives, cut in margarine until mixture resembles coarse crumbs. Sprinkle in water, 1 tablespoon at a time, mixing lightly with a fork after each addition until pastry just holds together. Cover dough and refrigerate 15 minutes. On lightly floured surface, roll pastry into 11-inch circle; cover loosely with plastic wrap and set aside.

Preheat oven to 425°.

Toss apples with combined ½ cup sugar and nutmeg; sprinkle with lemon juice. Set aside. Place ¼ cup sugar in 10-inch skillet with ovenproof handle. *Cook over medium heat until sugar melts and is golden brown, about 5 minutes, stirring occasionally. Add apple mixture and margarine; cook 5 minutes or until apples are just tender, stirring occasionally. Remove from heat.

Arrange apples in skillet so they are slightly mounded in the center. Place pastry on top of apples; tuck in edges. Cut slits in pastry to allow steam to escape. Bake 20 to 25 minutes or until lightly browned. Invert onto serving platter. Serve warm or at room temperature.

*Note: Watch carefully—the sugar can burn easily!

Nutritional Data

PER SERVING		EXCHANGES	
Calories:	200	Milk:	0.0
Fat (gm):	3.9	Veg.:	0.0
Cholesterol (mg):	0	Fruit:	1.5
Sodium (mg):	81	Bread:	1.0
Sat. fat (gm):	.6	Meat:	0.0
% Calories from fat:	17	Fat:	1.0

RASPBERRY-GLAZED BLUEBERRY TART

Imagine this tart, abundant with just-picked, perfectly ripe berries! Top helpings with a small scoop of low-fat frozen vanilla or lemon yogurt.

8 Servings

Basic Pie Crust (All-Purpose Flour, see Index)
1 tablespoon sugar
4 cups fresh blueberries
¾ cup raspberry spreadable fruit
1 tablespoon raspberry-flavor liqueur (optional)
2 teaspoons cornstarch
¼ teaspoon ground cinnamon
¼ teaspoon ground nutmeg

P reheat oven to 450°. Prepare pie crust, adding 1 tablespoon sugar to recipe and using 9-inch tart pan. Line pastry with weights, and bake until golden brown, 10 to 12 minutes. Cool on wire rack.

Arrange blueberries in cooled crust.

Combine spreadable fruit, liqueur, cornstarch, cinnamon, and nutmeg in small saucepan. Heat to boiling, stirring constantly. Remove from heat and spoon over blueberries. Refrigerate until glaze is slightly firm, about 30 minutes.

Nutritional Data

PER SERVING		EXCHANGES	
Calories:	169	Milk:	0.0
Fat (gm):	2.6	Veg.:	0.0
Cholesterol (mg):	0	Fruit:	1.0
Sodium (mg):	70	Bread:	1.0
Sat. fat (gm):	.4	Meat:	0.0
% Calories from fat:	13	Fat:	0.5

*PEAR TART WITH CRÈME ANGLAISE

Select pears that are just ripe, but not soft, for this elegant and delicate tart.

8 Servings

Basic Pie Crust (Cake Flour, see Index)
2 lbs. pears (4 large), peeled, cored, and sliced
¼ inch thick
¼ cup all-purpose flour
3 tablespoons sugar (substitute can be used, but
not aspartame*)
½ teaspoon ground cinnamon
¼ teaspoon ground nutmeg
Crème Anglaise (see Index)

P reheat oven to 375°. Prepare pie crust, using 9-inch tart pan.
Line pastry with weights, and bake 10 to 15 minutes or until
lightly browned. Cool on wire rack.
Toss pears with combined flour, sugar,* cinnamon, and nutmeg.
Arrange in overlapping circles in crust. Bake 20 to 25 minutes or until
pears are tender. Serve warm with Crème Anglaise.

Nutritional Data

PER SERVING			EXCHANGES		
Calories:	210	(187)	Milk:	0.0	
Fat (gm):	3.5		Veg.:	0.0	
Cholesterol (mg):	25	(27)	Fruit:	1.0	
Sodium (mg):	66	(69)	Bread:	2.0	(1.5)
Sat. fat (gm):	.6	(.7)	Meat:	0.0	
% Calories from fat:	14	(16)	Fat:	0.5	

(*Changes shown in parentheses will result from substituting 6
packets Sweet 'n Low® for sugar.)

3.
CHEESECAKES

Spring Berry
♦
New York-Style
♦
Lemon Meringue
♦
Chocolate Fillo

Spring Berry Cheesecake

You won't believe it until you taste it—delectable!

16 Servings

½ cup vanilla wafer cookie crumbs

2 tablespoons margarine, melted

1 cup low-fat cottage cheese

1 container (8 ozs.) non-fat cream cheese, softened

1 cup non-fat sour cream

⅓ cup sugar

3 eggs

½ cup skim milk

2 tablespoons lemon juice

3 tablespoons lemon rind, finely grated

3 tablespoons all-purpose flour

1 teaspoon vanilla

⅛ teaspoon salt

1 qt. strawberries or blueberries, sliced

¼ cup sugar

Preheat oven to 325°. Lightly grease 9-inch springform pan. Combine vanilla wafer crumbs and margarine and press in bottom of prepared pan.

Process cottage cheese in food processor or blender until smooth. Transfer cottage cheese to large bowl, add cream cheese, sour cream, and the ⅓ cup sugar and beat until light and fluffy. Add eggs one at a time, beating well after each addition. Stir in milk, lemon juice, lemon rind, flour, vanilla, and salt; blend well.

Pour into prepared crust and bake 50 minutes or until center is set. Cool on wire rack. Refrigerate 8 hours or overnight.

Combine berries and the ¼ cup sugar in medium bowl; cover and refrigerate. Spoon strawberries over individual cheesecake slices.

Nutritional Data

PER SERVING		EXCHANGES	
Calories:	126	Milk:	0.0
Fat (gm):	2.4	Veg.:	0.0
Cholesterol (mg):	46	Fruit:	0.0
Sodium (mg):	242	Bread:	1.0
Sat. fat (gm):	.6	Meat:	1.0
% Calories from fat:	18	Fat:	0.0

NEW YORK-STYLE CHEESECAKE

There is only one word for this cheesecake—spectacular!

12 Servings

Graham Cracker Crumb Crust (see Index)
2 containers (12 ozs. each) non-fat cream cheese, softened
¾ cup sugar
2 eggs
2 tablespoons cornstarch
1 teaspoon vanilla
1 cup reduced-fat sour cream

| P |

reheat oven to 350°. Make crumb crust, patting mixture on bottom and ½ inch up side of 9-inch springform pan. Increase oven temperature to 400°.

Beat cream cheese and sugar in large bowl until light and fluffy; beat in eggs, cornstarch, and vanilla. Add sour cream, mixing until well blended. Pour mixture into prepared crust.

Bake until cheesecake is set but still slightly soft in the center, 45 to 50 minutes. Turn oven off; let cheesecake cool in oven with door ajar for 3 hours. Refrigerate 8 hours or overnight.

Nutritional Data

PER SERVING		EXCHANGES	
Calories:	209	Milk:	0.0
Fat (gm):	6.2	Veg.:	0.0
Cholesterol (mg):	45	Fruit:	0.0
Sodium (mg):	452	Bread:	1.5
Sat. fat (gm):	3.2	Meat:	1.0
% Calories from fat:	28	Fat:	1.0

LEMON MERINGUE CHEESECAKE

Never has a cheesecake filling been quite as smooth and delicate as this. The filling is slightly soft, so chill very well before cutting.

12 Servings

Basic Pie Crust (All-Purpose Flour, see Index)
2 containers (12 ozs. each) non-fat cream cheese, softened
4 egg yolks
⅔ cup lemon juice
2 tablespoons flour
1 cup sugar
⅓ cup cornstarch
⅔ cup water
2 teaspoons lemon rind, grated
4 egg whites
¼ teaspoon cream of tartar
⅓ cup powdered sugar

Preheat oven to 400°. Prepare pie crust, using 9-inch pie pan. Line pastry with weights and bake until golden, 12 to 15 minutes. Cool on wire rack.

Beat cream cheese and egg yolks in medium bowl until smooth; beat in lemon juice and flour.

Mix sugar and cornstarch in medium saucepan; stir in water and lemon rind. Cook over medium heat, stirring constantly, until mixture thickens and boils; boil 1 minute, stirring constantly. Remove from heat. Gradually stir in cheese mixture, mixing until completely blended. Pour hot mixture into prepared crust.

Beat egg whites and cream of tartar in large bowl until foamy. Gradually beat in powdered sugar, beating to stiff but not dry peaks. Spread meringue over top of pie, sealing it to edge of crust. Bake at 400° until meringue is golden, about 10 minutes. Cool to room temperature on wire rack; refrigerate at least 4 hours before serving.

Nutritional Data

PER SERVING		EXCHANGES	
Calories:	224	Milk:	0.0
Fat (gm):	3.3	Veg.:	0.0
Cholesterol (mg):	81	Fruit:	0.0
Sodium (mg):	441	Bread:	2.5
Sat. fat (gm):	.8	Meat:	1.0
% Calories from fat:	13	Fat:	0.0

CHOCOLATE FILLO CHEESECAKE

The fillo pastry is unusual and attractive, making this chocolate cheesecake unique.

12 Servings

- 2 tablespoons unseasoned dry breadcrumbs
- 6 sheets frozen fillo pastry, thawed
- 2 containers (12 ozs. each) non-fat cream cheese, softened
- 1 cup reduced-fat sour cream
- ⅔ cup sugar
- ⅓ cup Dutch process (unsweetened) cocoa
- 2 eggs
- 3 tablespoons flour
- ½ teaspoon ground cinnamon

Preheat oven to 375°. Lightly grease 9-inch springform pan with cooking spray; sprinkle with breadcrumbs.

Working quickly, spray each fillo sheet lightly with cooking spray. Layer fillo in bottom of pan, turning each slightly so that corners are staggered. Bake 6 to 8 minutes or until lightly browned. Cool on wire rack.

Reduce oven temperature to 350°.

Beat cream cheese until fluffy in large bowl; mix in sour cream, sugar, and cocoa. Beat in eggs; mix in flour and cinnamon. Pour mixture into fillo crust; gently fold edges of fillo inward so that edges of fillo do not extend outside of pan.

Bake 50 minutes or until center of cheesecake is almost set. Cover edges of fillo crust with aluminum foil during last 15 or 20 minutes of baking time if beginning to get too brown.

Cool on wire rack 10 minutes. Carefully remove side of pan; cool to room temperature. Cover loosely and refrigerate 8 hours or overnight.

Nutritional Data

PER SERVING		EXCHANGES	
Calories:	159	Milk:	0.0
Fat (gm):	1.4	Veg.:	0.0
Cholesterol (mg):	45	Fruit:	0.0
Sodium (mg):	358	Bread:	1.0
Sat. fat (gm):	.3	Meat:	1.5
% Calories from fat:	8	Fat:	0.0

4.
COOKIES

Gingersnappers

Chocolate Crinkles

Cinnamon Oatmeal Cookies

Favorite Sugar Cookies

Glazed Chocolate Shortbread Squares

Cardamom Crisps

Chocolate-Glazed Cookie Crisps

Chewy Cocoa Brownies

Sugared Lemon Squares

Fig and Pear Bars

Chocolate Fudge Meringues

Orange-Almond Meringues

Peppermint Clouds

Hazelnut Macaroons

Anise-Almond Biscotti

Apricot-Sesame Biscotti

45

GINGERSNAPPERS

Dry mustard and black pepper are the "secret" ingredients that add the zesty flavor to these ginger favorites.

54 Cookies (1 per serving)

8 tablespoons margarine, softened
¾ cup packed light brown sugar
¼ cup light molasses
1 egg
2 cups all-purpose flour
1 teaspoon baking soda
1 teaspoon ground cinnamon
1 teaspoon ground ginger
½ teaspoon ground cloves
½ teaspoon dry mustard
¼ teaspoon ground black pepper
3 tablespoons granulated sugar

Beat margarine and brown sugar until fluffy in large bowl; mix in molasses and egg. Mix in combined flour, baking soda, cinnamon, ginger, cloves, mustard, and pepper. Refrigerate, covered, 2 to 3 hours.

Preheat oven to 350°.

Measure granulated sugar into pie pan or shallow bowl. Drop dough by teaspoons into sugar and roll into balls. (Dough will be sticky.) Place cookies on greased cookie sheets; flatten with fork or bottom of glass. Bake until firm to touch, 8 to 10 minutes. Cool on wire rack.

Nutritional Data

PER SERVING		EXCHANGES	
Calories:	43	Milk:	0.0
Fat (gm):	1	Veg.:	0.0
Cholesterol (mg):	4	Fruit:	0.0
Sodium (mg):	37	Bread:	0.5
Sat. fat (gm):	.2	Meat:	0.0
% Calories from fat:	20	Fat:	0.0

CHOCOLATE CRINKLES

These cookies have crinkled, crisp tops and are soft inside.

---

54 Cookies (1 per serving)

7 tablespoons margarine, softened
1¼ cups packed light brown sugar
⅓ cup low-fat plain yogurt, or sour cream
2 egg whites
1 teaspoon vanilla
1¾ cups all-purpose flour
¾ cup unsweetened cocoa
1 teaspoon baking soda
1 teaspoon ground cinnamon
¼ cup granulated sugar

In large bowl, beat margarine and brown sugar until fluffy. Mix in yogurt, egg whites, and vanilla. Mix in combined flour, cocoa, baking soda, and cinnamon. Refrigerate, covered, 2 to 3 hours.

Preheat oven to 350°.

Measure granulated sugar into pie pan or shallow bowl. Drop dough by tablespoons into sugar and roll into balls. (Dough will be soft.) Place cookies on greased cookie sheets; flatten with fork or bottom of glass. Bake until firm to touch, 10 to 12 minutes. Cool on wire racks.

Nutritional Data

PER SERVING		EXCHANGES	
Calories:	48	Milk:	0.0
Fat (gm):	1	Veg.:	0.0
Cholesterol (mg):	0	Fruit:	0.0
Sodium (mg):	37	Bread:	0.5
Sat. fat (gm):	.2	Meat:	0.0
% Calories from fat:	18	Fat:	0.0

CINNAMON OATMEAL COOKIES

Old fashioned favorites!

42 Cookies (1 per serving)

- 5 tablespoons margarine, softened
- ¼ cup low-fat plain yogurt
- 2 egg whites
- 1 teaspoon vanilla
- 1 cup packed light brown sugar
- 1 cup all-purpose flour
- 1¼ cups quick-cooking oats
- ½ teaspoon baking soda
- ¼ teaspoon baking powder
- 1 teaspoon ground cinnamon
- ¼ teaspoon salt

Preheat oven to 375°.

In large bowl, beat margarine, yogurt, egg whites, and vanilla until smooth. Mix in brown sugar. Mix in combined flour, oats, baking soda, baking powder, cinnamon, and salt.

Drop mixture by tablespoons onto greased cookie sheets. Bake until cookies are lightly browned, 10 to 12 minutes. Cool on wire racks.

Nutritional Data

PER SERVING		EXCHANGES	
Calories:	47	Milk:	0.0
Fat (gm):	.9	Veg.:	0.0
Cholesterol (mg):	0	Fruit:	0.0
Sodium (mg):	45	Bread:	0.5
Sat. fat (gm):	.1	Meat:	0.0
% Calories from fat:	17	Fat:	0.0

FAVORITE SUGAR COOKIES

Moist and slightly chewy—please don't overbake! Ground cinnamon can be substituted for the nutmeg if you like.

36 Cookies (1 per serving)

4 tablespoons margarine, softened
⅔ cup sugar
1 egg
1½ tablespoons lemon juice
1½ cups all-purpose flour
½ teaspoon baking soda
½ teaspoon ground nutmeg
Granulated sugar

Preheat oven to 375°. In medium-size bowl, beat margarine until fluffy. Beat in ⅔ cup sugar, egg, and lemon juice. Mix in combined flour, baking soda, and nutmeg.

Roll dough into ¾-inch balls; roll balls in granulated sugar and place on ungreased cookie sheets. Flatten to 2 inch diameter with bottom of glass. Bake until beginning to brown, about 10 minutes. Cool on wire racks.

Nutritional Data

PER SERVING		EXCHANGES	
Calories:	40	Milk:	0.0
Fat (gm):	.8	Veg.:	0.0
Cholesterol (mg):	6	Fruit:	0.0
Sodium (mg):	28	Bread:	0.5
Sat. fat (gm):	.2	Meat:	0.0
% Calories from fat:	18	Fat:	0.0

GLAZED CHOCOLATE SHORTBREAD SQUARES

Rich, chocolatey, and crisp!

60 Cookies (1 per serving)

Shortbread
- 1½ cups all-purpose flour
- ¼ cup unsweetened cocoa
- ½ cup sugar
- ¼ teaspoon salt
- 8 tablespoons margarine, softened
- 1 egg
- 2 teaspoons vanilla

Sugar Glaze
- 2 cups powdered sugar
- 2 tablespoons margarine, softened
- 2-3 tablespoons skim milk

Shortbread: Preheat oven to 350°.

Combine flour, cocoa, sugar, and salt in medium-size bowl; cut in margarine with pastry blender or 2 knives until mixture resembles coarse crumbs. Mix in egg and vanilla, stirring just enough to form a soft dough.

Place dough in bottom of greased jelly roll pan, 15 × 10 inches. Pat and spread dough, using fingers and small spatula, until bottom of pan is evenly covered. Pierce dough with tines of fork.

Bake until firm to touch, 20 to 25 minutes. Cool slightly on wire rack.

Sugar Glaze: In a small bowl, mix powdered sugar and margarine until smooth. Stir in enough milk to make glaze consistency. Spoon glaze over shortbread, and cut into squares while warm.

Nutritional Data

PER SERVING		EXCHANGES	
Calories:	41	Milk:	0.0
Fat (gm):	1.1	Veg.:	0.0
Cholesterol (mg):	4	Fruit:	0.0
Sodium (mg):	32	Bread:	0.5
Sat. fat (gm):	.2	Meat:	0.0
% Calories from fat:	24	Fat:	0.0

CARDAMOM CRISPS

For flavor variations, ground cinnamon or allspice can be substituted for the cardamom. These cookies require some care in spreading in the pan but are well worth the effort!

60 Cookies (1 per serving)

Crisps
- 1¾ cups all-purpose flour
- ½ cup sugar
- 1½ teaspoons ground cardamom
- ¼ teaspoon salt
- 8 tablespoons margarine, softened
- 1 egg
- 1 teaspoon vanilla
- 1 egg white, beaten

Vanilla Glaze
- 1 cup powdered sugar
- 2 tablespoons margarine, melted
- 1 teaspoon vanilla
- 1-2 tablespoons skim milk

Crisps: Preheat oven to 350°.

Combine flour, sugar, cardamom, and salt in medium-size bowl; cut in margarine with pastry blender or 2 knives until mixture resembles coarse crumbs. Mix in whole egg and vanilla, stirring just enough to form a soft dough.

Place dough in bottom of greased jelly roll pan, 15 × 10 inches. Pat and spread dough, using fingers and small spatula or knife, until bottom of pan is evenly covered. Brush dough with beaten egg white.

Bake until edges of cookies are lightly browned, 20 to 25 minutes. Cool in pan several minutes.

Vanilla Glaze: Mix powdered sugar and margarine with vanilla and enough milk to make glaze consistency. Drizzle glaze over warm cookies and cut into squares.

Nutritional Data

PER SERVING		EXCHANGES	
Calories:	36	Milk:	0.0
Fat (gm):	1.1	Veg.:	0.0
Cholesterol (mg):	3	Fruit:	0.0
Sodium (mg):	33	Bread:	0.5
Sat. fat (gm):	.2	Meat:	0.0
% Calories from fat:	27	Fat:	0.0

CHOCOLATE-GLAZED COOKIE CRISPS

Bake cookie crisps only until beginning to brown, and cut while warm for best results.

60 Cookies (1 per serving)

Cookies

1¾ cups all-purpose flour
½ cup packed light brown sugar
¼ teaspoon salt
8 tablespoons margarine, softened
1 egg
1 teaspoon vanilla

Chocolate Glaze

1 egg white, beaten
1 cup powdered sugar
2 tablespoons unsweetened cocoa
2 tablespoons margarine, melted
1-2 tablespoons skim milk

Cookies: Preheat oven to 350°.

Combine flour, brown sugar, and salt in medium-size bowl; cut in margarine with pastry blender or 2 knives until mixture resembles coarse crumbs. Mix in whole egg and vanilla, stirring just enough to form a soft dough.

Place dough in bottom of greased jelly roll pan, 15 × 10 inches. Pat and spread dough, using fingers and small spatula or knife, until bottom of pan is evenly covered. Brush dough with beaten egg white.

Bake until edges of cookies are lightly browned, 20 to 25 minutes. Cool in pan several minutes.

Chocolate Glaze: Mix powdered sugar and cocoa in small bowl. Mix in margarine and enough milk to make glaze consistency. Drizzle glaze over warm cookies and cut into squares.

Nutritional Data

PER SERVING		EXCHANGES	
Calories:	37	Milk:	0.0
Fat (gm):	1.1	Veg.:	0.0
Cholesterol (mg):	3	Fruit:	0.0
Sodium (mg):	33	Bread:	0.5
Sat. fat (gm):	.2	Meat:	0.0
% Calories from fat:	26	Fat:	0.0

CHEWEY COCOA BROWNIES

◆

You never knew a "skinny" brownie could be this good! And so low fat.

◆

25 Brownies (1 per serving)

1 cup all-purpose flour
1 cup sugar
¼ cup unsweetened cocoa
5 tablespoons margarine, melted
¼ cup skim milk
1 egg
2 egg whites
¼ cup honey
1 teaspoon vanilla

P reheat oven to 350°.

Mix flour, sugar, and cocoa in medium-size bowl. Stir in margarine, milk, egg, egg whites, honey, and vanilla until smooth. Pour mixture into greased and floured 8 × 8-inch baking pan.

Bake until brownies spring back when touched and begin to pull away from sides of pan, about 30 minutes. Cool completely on wire rack; cut into squares.

◆

Nutritional Data

PER SERVING		EXCHANGES	
Calories:	75	Milk:	0.0
Fat (gm):	1.5	Veg.:	0.0
Cholesterol (mg):	8	Fruit:	0.0
Sodium (mg):	35	Bread:	1.0
Sat. fat (gm):	.3	Meat:	0.0
% Calories from fat:	18	Fat:	0.0

◆

SUGARED LEMON SQUARES

Just like the favorites you remember—but much "skinnier"!

25 Squares (1 per serving)

¾ cup all-purpose flour
4 tablespoons margarine, softened
2 tablespoons reduced-fat sour cream
2 tablespoons granulated sugar
1 cup granulated sugar
1 egg
2 egg whites
1 tablespoon lemon rind, grated
3 tablespoons lemon juice
½ teaspoon baking powder
¼ teaspoon salt
   Powdered sugar

P reheat oven to 350°.
    Mix flour, margarine, sour cream, and 2 tablespoons granulated sugar in small bowl to form soft dough. Pat dough into bottom and ¼ inch up sides of 8 × 8-inch baking pan. Bake until lightly browned, about 20 minutes. Cool on wire rack.
    Mix 1 cup granulated sugar and remaining ingredients, except powdered sugar, in small bowl; pour over baked pastry. Bake until no indentation remains when touched in the center, 20 to 25 minutes. Cool on wire rack; cut into squares. Sprinkle lightly with powdered sugar.

Nutritional Data

PER SERVING		EXCHANGES	
Calories:	61	Milk:	0.0
Fat (gm):	1.3	Veg.:	0.0
Cholesterol (mg):	8	Fruit:	0.0
Sodium (mg):	57	Bread:	1.0
Sat. fat (gm):	.4	Meat:	0.0
% Calories from fat:	19	Fat:	0.0

*FIG AND PEAR BARS

Chewy, dense, and oh, so good! A fruit bar at its best.

30 Bars (1 per serving)

¾ cup dried figs, chopped
¾ cup dried pears, chopped
½ cup water
2 tablespoons packed light brown sugar
  (substitute can be used, but not aspartame*)
5 tablespoons margarine, softened
2 tablespoons granulated sugar (substitute can
  be used, but not aspartame*)
3 egg whites
1 teaspoon vanilla
1¾ cups all-purpose flour
½ teaspoon baking soda
¼ teaspoon salt
2 tablespoons 2% milk

In small saucepan, heat figs, pears, water, and brown sugar* to boiling. Reduce heat and simmer, uncovered, until fruit is softened and mixture is thick, about 20 minutes. Process mixture in food processor or blender until smooth. Cool.

Beat margarine and granulated sugar* in medium-size bowl until fluffy; beat in egg whites and vanilla. Mix in combined flour, baking soda, and salt. Shape dough into 4 logs, each about 5 × 2 × ½ inches. Wrap each in plastic wrap and refrigerate about 1 hour.

Preheat oven to 400°.

Roll 1 log on floured surface into 12 × 5-inch flat rectangle. Using ¼ of the fruit mixture, spread a 1-inch strip down center of dough. Fold sides of dough over the filling, pressing edges to seal. Cut log in half and place, seam side down, on greased cookie sheet. Repeat with remaining dough logs and filling. Brush top of logs with milk.

Bake until lightly browned, about 12 minutes. Cool on wire racks; cut into 1½-inch bars.

Nutritional Data

PER SERVING			EXCHANGES	
Calories:	68	(63)	Milk:	0.0
Fat (gm):	1.1		Veg.:	0.0
Cholesterol (mg):	0		Fruit:	0.5
Sodium (mg):	60	(61)	Bread:	0.5
Sat. fat (gm):	.2		Meat:	0.0
% Calories from fat:	14	(16)	Fat:	0.0

(*Changes in parentheses will result from substituting a total of 6 packets of Sweet 'n Low® for sugar.)

CHOCOLATE FUDGE MERINGUES

Better bake several batches—these won't last long!

24 Cookies (1 per serving)

3 egg whites
⅛ teaspoon cream of tartar
¼ teaspoon salt
2 cups powdered sugar
⅓ cup unsweetened cocoa
1 oz. semi-sweet chocolate, finely chopped

P reheat oven to 300°.

In medium-size bowl, beat egg whites until foamy. Add cream of tartar and salt; beat to soft peaks. Beat in sugar gradually, beating until mixture forms stiff, shiny peaks. Fold in cocoa; fold in chopped chocolate.

Drop mixture by tablespoons onto parchment- or aluminum-foil-lined cookie sheets. Bake at 300° until cookies feel crisp when touched, 20 to 25 minutes. Cool in pans on wire racks.

Nutritional Data

PER SERVING		EXCHANGES	
Calories:	43	Milk:	0.0
Fat (gm):	.5	Veg.:	0.0
Cholesterol (mg):	0	Fruit:	0.0
Sodium (mg):	29	Bread:	0.5
Sat. fat (gm):	0	Meat:	0.0
% Calories from fat:	11	Fat:	0.0

ORANGE-ALMOND MERINGUES

◆

Party perfect!

24 Cookies (1 per serving)

3 egg whites
½ teaspoon orange extract
⅛ teaspoon cream of tartar
¼ teaspoon salt
¾ cup sugar
⅓ cup toasted almonds, chopped

P reheat oven to 300°.

In medium-size bowl, beat egg whites until foamy. Add orange extract, cream of tartar, and salt; beat to soft peaks. Beat in sugar gradually, beating until mixture forms stiff, shiny peaks. Fold in almonds.

Drop mixture by tablespoons onto parchment- or aluminum-foil-lined cookie sheets. Bake until cookies begin to brown and feel crisp when touched, 20 to 25 minutes. Cool in pans on wire racks.

◆

Nutritional Data

PER SERVING		EXCHANGES	
Calories:	34	Milk:	0.0
Fat (gm):	.8	Veg.:	0.0
Cholesterol (mg):	0	Fruit:	0.0
Sodium (mg):	29	Bread:	0.5
Sat. fat (gm):	.1	Meat:	0.0
% Calories from fat:	21	Fat:	0.0

PEPPERMINT CLOUDS

Although wonderful cookies any time, peppermint always reminds me of Christmas holidays.

24 Cookies (1 per serving)

3 egg whites
⅛ teaspoon cream of tartar
¼ teaspoon salt
¾ cup sugar
⅓ cup (2 ozs.) peppermint candies, crushed

P reheat oven to 300°.
    In medium-size bowl, beat egg whites until foamy. Add cream of tartar and salt; beat to soft peaks. Beat in sugar gradually, beating until mixture forms stiff, shiny peaks. Reserve 2 tablespoons crushed candy; fold remaining candy into egg white mixture.
    Drop mixture by tablespoons onto parchment- or aluminum-foil-lined cookie sheets. Sprinkle tops of cookies with reserved candy. Bake until cookies begin to brown and feel crisp when touched, 20 to 25 minutes. Cool in pans on wire racks.

Nutritional Data

PER SERVING		EXCHANGES	
Calories:	34	Milk:	0.0
Fat (gm):	0	Veg.:	0.0
Cholesterol (mg):	0	Fruit:	0.0
Sodium (mg):	30	Bread:	0.5
Sat. fat (gm):	0	Meat:	0.0
% Calories from fat:	0	Fat:	0.0

HAZELNUT MACAROONS

Use any favorite nuts in these moist and crunchy macaroons.

30 Cookies (1 per serving)

4 egg whites
⅛ teaspoon cream of tartar
¼ teaspoon salt
1 cup sugar
1 cup canned sweetened coconut
¼ cup hazelnuts or pecans, finely chopped

P reheat oven to 300°.

In medium-size bowl, beat egg whites until foamy. Add cream of tartar and salt; beat to soft peaks. Beat in sugar gradually, beating until mixture forms stiff, shiny peaks. Fold in coconut; fold in hazelnuts.

Drop mixture by tablespoons onto parchment- or aluminum-foil-lined cookie sheets. Bake until cookies begin to brown and feel crisp when touched, 20 to 25 minutes. Cool in pans on wire racks.

Nutritional Data

PER SERVING		EXCHANGES	
Calories:	44	Milk:	0.0
Fat (gm):	1.4	Veg.:	0.0
Cholesterol (mg):	0	Fruit:	0.0
Sodium (mg):	25.6	Bread:	0.5
Sat. fat (gm):	.8	Meat:	0.0
% Calories from fat:	28	Fat:	0.5

ANISE-ALMOND BISCOTTI

Crisp biscotti are perfect for dunking into coffee, tea—or Vin Santo, the Italian way!

60 Bars (1 per serving)

4 tablespoons margarine, softened
¾ cup sugar
2 eggs
2 egg whites
2½ cups all-purpose flour
2 teaspoons anise seed, crushed
1½ teaspoons baking powder
½ teaspoon baking soda
¼ teaspoon salt
⅓ cup whole blanched almonds

| **P** | reheat oven to 350°. In medium-size bowl, beat margarine, sugar, eggs, and egg whites until smooth. Mix in combined |

flour, anise seed, baking powder, baking soda, and salt. Mix in almonds.

Shape dough on greased cookie sheets into 4 slightly flattened rolls 1½ inches in diameter. Bake until lightly browned, about 20 minutes. Let stand on wire rack until cool enough to handle; cut bars into ½-inch slices.

Arrange slices, cut sides down, on ungreased cookie sheets. Bake until toasted on the bottom, 7 to 10 minutes; turn and bake until biscotti are golden on the bottom and feel almost dry, 7 to 10 minutes. Cool on wire racks.

Nutritional Data

PER SERVING		EXCHANGES	
Calories:	38	Milk:	0.0
Fat (gm):	.9	Veg.:	0.0
Cholesterol (mg):	7	Fruit:	0.0
Sodium (mg):	37	Bread:	0.5
Sat. fat (gm):	.2	Meat:	0.0
% Calories from fat:	22	Fat:	0.0

APRICOT-SESAME BISCOTTI

Biscotti become crisper as they cool, so bake only until almost dry.

60 Bars (1 per serving)

2½ cups all-purpose flour
1 teaspoon baking powder
½ teaspoon baking soda
¾ cup packed light brown sugar
2 tablespoons orange rind, grated
2 tablespoons sesame seed, toasted
2 eggs
2 egg whites

Preheat oven to 350°.

Combine flour, baking powder, baking soda, brown sugar, orange rind, and sesame seed in large bowl. Mix eggs and egg whites; stir into flour mixture until smooth.

Shape dough on greased cookie sheets into 4 slightly flattened rolls, 1½ inches in diameter. Bake until lightly browned, about 20 minutes. Let stand on wire rack until cool enough to handle; cut bars into ½-inch slices.

Arrange slices, cut sides down, on ungreased cookie sheets. Bake until toasted on the bottom, 7 to 10 minutes; turn and bake until biscotti are golden on the bottom and feel almost dry, 7 to 10 minutes. Cool on wire racks.

Nutritional Data

PER SERVING		EXCHANGES	
Calories:	34	Milk:	0.0
Fat (gm):	.4	Veg.:	0.0
Cholesterol (mg):	7	Fruit:	0.0
Sodium (mg):	17	Bread:	0.5
Sat. fat (gm):	.1	Meat:	0.0
% Calories from fat:	10	Fat:	0.0

5.
FRESH FRUIT DESSERTS

Spiced Orange Compote

Honey-Lime Melon Wedges

Honey-Broiled Pineapple Slices

Fresh Berry Rhubarb

Wine-Poached Plums

Caramel Apple Slices

Bananas Foster

Mixed Fruit Kabobs

Strawberry-Kiwi Shortcake

Apple-Cranberry Crisp

Cherry-Berry Grunt

Pears Belle Hélène

Baked Fruit Compote

Tropical Fruit Soup

Sweet Cherry Soup

SPICED ORANGE COMPOTE

A perfect dessert for winter, when many fresh fruits are not yet available. Serve with cookies—Cardamom Crisps would bring smiles.

8 Servings

- 5 oranges, peeled, sliced
- ⅓ cup orange juice
- 3 tablespoons packed light brown sugar
- 2-3 tablespoons orange-flavor liqueur
- 4 whole allspice
- 1 cinnamon stick
- Mint sprigs

Place oranges in shallow glass bowl. Mix orange juice, brown sugar, orange liqueur, allspice, and cinnamon in small saucepan. Heat just to boiling; pour over orange slices. Refrigerate, covered, 8 hours or overnight for flavors to blend. Garnish with mint.

Nutritional Data

PER SERVING		EXCHANGES	
Calories:	74	Milk:	0.0
Fat (gm):	.1	Veg.:	0.0
Cholesterol (mg):	0	Fruit:	1.0
Sodium (mg):	2	Bread:	0.0
Sat. fat (gm):	0	Meat:	0.0
% Calories from fat:	1	Fat:	0.0

HONEY-LIME MELON WEDGES

A recipe that is so simple, but so very good.

4 Servings

  1 small cantaloupe, or other melon in season
3-4 tablespoons honey
  4 lime wedges
     Ground nutmeg

 ut melon into wedges. Drizzle honey over melon, squeeze lime wedges over each slice, and sprinkle with nutmeg.

Nutritional Data

PER SERVING		EXCHANGES	
Calories:	112	Milk:	0.0
Fat (gm):	.5	Veg.:	0.0
Cholesterol (mg):	0	Fruit:	2.0
Sodium (mg):	15	Bread:	0.0
Sat. fat (gm):	.0	Meat:	0.0
% Calories from fat:	3	Fat:	0.0

HONEY-BROILED PINEAPPLE SLICES

This dessert beckons a selection of cookie accompaniments: choose among Chewy Chocolate Brownies, Fig and Pear Bars, or Hazelnut Macaroons (see Index).

4 Servings (2 pineapple slices each)

1 medium pineapple (1½ lbs.), peeled, cored, and cut into eight ½-inch slices
3 tablespoons honey
2 tablespoons frozen orange juice concentrate, thawed
2 tablespoons fresh cilantro or mint, minced

P reheat broiler to medium-high. Arrange pineapple rings on broiler pan. Combine honey and orange concentrate in small bowl; brush onto pineapple.

Broil, 6 inches from heat source, 3 minutes; turn and baste with honey mixture. Broil 2 to 3 minutes more or until golden. Sprinkle with cilantro.

Nutritional Data

PER SERVING		EXCHANGES	
Calories:	143	Milk:	0.0
Fat (gm):	.7	Veg.:	0.0
Cholesterol (mg):	0	Fruit:	2.5
Sodium (mg):	3	Bread:	0.0
Sat. fat (gm):	0	Meat:	0.0
% Calories from fat:	4	Fat:	0.0

*FRESH BERRY RHUBARB

Frozen rhubarb can also be used so you can enjoy this light dessert all year. Calories are "skinny," so you might wish to add a sweet from the cookie chapter.

---

6 Servings (½ cup each)

½ cup sugar (substitute can be used*)
½ cup water
4 cups rhubarb (about 1 lb.), sliced
¼ teaspoon ground cinnamon
1 cup strawberries, sliced
1 cup blueberries

C ombine sugar* and water in medium-size saucepan. Heat to boiling; reduce heat and add rhubarb. Simmer, uncovered, 10 minutes or until rhubarb is tender, stirring occasionally. Remove from heat and stir in cinnamon; cool completely. Stir in strawberries and blueberries.

Note: If using sweeteners with aspartame, stir into fruit after it has been cooked and cooled slightly.

Nutritional Data

PER SERVING			EXCHANGES	
Calories:	98	(46)	Milk:	0.0
Fat (gm):	.3		Veg.:	0.0
Cholesterol (mg):	0		Fruit:	1.5 (1.0)
Sodium (mg):	5		Bread:	0.0
Sat. fat (gm):	0		Meat:	0.0
% Calories from fat:	3	(6)	Fat:	0.0

(*Changes shown in parentheses will result from substituting 12 packets Equal® for sugar.)

WINE-POACHED PLUMS

White port wine is unique in this recipe, but red port can be used if you prefer.

4 Servings

     2 cups white port wine
⅓-½ cup sugar
     1 cinnamon stick
     1 whole nutmeg
   12 medium plums

[C] ombine wine, sugar, cinnamon, and nutmeg in medium-size saucepan. Heat to boiling, add plums, and reduce heat to low. Gently simmer plums, covered, 10 to 15 minutes or until tender. Remove plums to serving dish.

Bring poaching liquid to a boil over high heat. Boil gently 12 to 15 minutes or until slightly thickened. Serve over plums.

Nutritional Data

PER SERVING		EXCHANGES	
Calories:	247	Milk:	0.0
Fat (gm):	1.2	Veg.:	0.0
Cholesterol (mg):	0	Fruit:	4.0
Sodium (mg):	5	Bread:	0.0
Sat. fat (gm):	.1	Meat:	0.0
% Calories from fat:	4	Fat:	0.0

CARAMEL APPLE SLICES

Serve these fragrant apple slices over low-fat frozen vanilla yogurt for a sumptuous sundae, or serve over pancakes, waffles, or crepes.

4 Servings

  2 large apples (sweet or tart)
  ½ cup apple cider
  ¼ cup packed light brown sugar
     Ground cinnamon
     Ground nutmeg

| C | ut apples into fourths and core. Cut apples further into scant ¼-inch slices and place in medium-size skillet. Pour apple cider over; sprinkle with brown sugar. Heat to boiling; reduce heat and simmer, uncovered, until apples are crisp-tender, 3 to 4 minutes. Remove apples to serving dish with slotted spoon.

    Heat cider mixture to boiling; boil until mixture is reduced to a syrup consistency. Pour syrup over apples, and sprinkle very lightly with cinnamon and nutmeg.

Note: Apples can be sliced in advance. Rinse them in 1 cup water mixed with 2 tablespoons lemon juice to prevent apples from turning brown.

Nutritional Data

PER SERVING		EXCHANGES	
Calories:	104	Milk:	0.0
Fat (gm):	.3	Veg.:	0.0
Cholesterol (mg):	0	Fruit:	1.5
Sodium (mg):	5	Bread:	0.0
Sat. fat (gm):	0	Meat:	0.0
% Calories from fat:	2	Fat:	0.0

BANANAS FOSTER

A taste of New Orleans!

4 Servings

¼ cup packed light brown sugar
1½ teaspoons cornstarch
½ cup water
1 tablespoon rum
1 teaspoon vanilla
2 medium bananas, peeled and sliced
¼ cup toasted pecan halves
1⅓ cups frozen low-fat vanilla yogurt

Mix brown sugar and cornstarch in small saucepan; stir in water. Cook over medium heat until thickened, stirring constantly. Reduce heat to low; stir in rum and vanilla. Gently stir in bananas and simmer 1 to 2 minutes or until bananas are warm; stir in pecans. Serve warm over frozen yogurt.

Nutritional Data

PER SERVING		EXCHANGES	
Calories:	236	Milk:	0.0
Fat (gm):	5.5	Veg.:	0.0
Cholesterol (mg):	0	Fruit:	2.0
Sodium (mg):	5	Bread:	1.0
Sat. fat (gm):	.5	Meat:	0.0
% Calories from fat:	20	Fat:	1.0

MIXED FRUIT KABOBS WITH RASPBERRY SAUCE

Orange Marmalade Sauce and Honey Sauce (see Index) are also excellent choices for these fruit kabobs; or offer a selection of sauces.

8 Servings (2 kabobs per serving)

2 bananas
2 kiwi fruit, peeled
2 peaches, pitted
2 pears, cored
  Vegetable cooking spray
¼ cup apple or orange juice
  Summer Raspberry Coulis (see Index)

C ut each piece of fruit into 8 equal pieces. Alternately thread fruit onto sixteen 6-inch wooden or metal skewers.

Coat a grill or broiling pan with non-stick cooking spray. Grill or broil, 6 inches from medium-hot heat source, 5 to 8 minutes or until bananas are golden, rotating kabobs occasionally. Baste with apple juice. Serve with Summer Raspberry Coulis.

Nutritional Data

PER SERVING		EXCHANGES	
Calories:	110	Milk:	0.0
Fat (gm):	.6	Veg.:	0.0
Cholesterol (mg):	0	Fruit:	2.0
Sodium (mg):	1	Bread:	0.0
Sat. fat (gm):	0	Meat:	0.0
% Calories from fat:	5	Fat:	0.0

*STRAWBERRY-KIWI SHORTCAKE

This moist, nutritious whole-wheat shortcake is made to order for a duo of fresh fruit.

8 Servings

  1 cup all-purpose flour
  1 cup whole-wheat flour
  ⅓ cup sugar (substitute can be used, but not
    aspartame*)
1½ teaspoons baking powder
  ½ teaspoon baking soda
  ¼ teaspoon salt
  ⅔ cup buttermilk
  4 tablespoons margarine, melted
  1 egg
  2 egg whites
1½ teaspoons vanilla
  3 cups strawberries, sliced
  1 cup kiwi fruit, peeled, sliced

P reheat oven to 400°.

Combine flours, sugar,* baking powder, baking soda, and salt in medium-size bowl. Mix buttermilk, margarine, egg, egg whites, and vanilla in small bowl until smooth; stir into flour mixture, mixing only until dry ingredients are moistened.

With floured hands, lightly pat dough into lightly greased 8-inch (round or square) baking pan. Bake 12 to 15 minutes or until toothpick inserted near center comes out clean. Cool on wire rack 10 minutes. Slice into wedges or squares and top with strawberries and kiwi fruit.

Nutritional Data

PER SERVING			EXCHANGES		
Calories:	216	(190)	Milk:	0.0	
Fat (gm):	4.4		Veg.:	0.0	
Cholesterol (mg):	27		Fruit:	0.5	(0.0)
Sodium (mg):	290	(294)	Bread:	1.5	(2.0)
Sat. fat (gm):	.9		Meat:	0.5	(0.0)
% Calories from fat:	18	(20)	Fat:	1.0	

(*Changes in parentheses will result from substituting 8 packets of Sweet 'n Low® for sugar.)

*APPLE-CRANBERRY CRISP

Apples and cranberries are happy companions in this streusel-topped fruit crisp.

6 Servings

Fruit Filling
2½ lbs. cooking apples, peeled, cored, and sliced
1 cup fresh or frozen cranberries, thawed
½ cup packed light brown sugar (substitute can be used, but not aspartame*)
2 tablespoons flour
1 teaspoon crystallized ginger, finely chopped

Streusel Topping
⅓ cup quick-cooking oats
3 tablespoons flour
3 tablespoons packed light brown sugar (substitute can be used, but not aspartame*)
1½ tablespoons margarine

Fruit Filling: Preheat oven to 350°.
Combine apples, cranberries, brown sugar,* flour, and ginger in a 1-quart glass casserole.
Streusel Topping: In small bowl, combine all ingredients until crumbly. Sprinkle onto confection. Bake, uncovered, 30 to 40 minutes or until apples are tender. Serve warm.

Nutritional Data

PER SERVING			EXCHANGES	
Calories:	223	(140)	Milk:	0.0
Fat (gm):	2.2		Veg.:	0.0
Cholesterol (mg):	0		Fruit:	3.0 (1.5)
Sodium (mg):	41	(45)	Bread:	0.5
Sat. fat (gm):	.4		Meat:	0.0
% Calories from fat:	9	(13)	Fat:	0.5

(*Changes shown in parentheses will result from substituting a total of 16½ packets Sweet 'n Low® for sugar.)

CHERRY-BERRY GRUNT

A wonderful campfire dessert brought indoors and given a cherry accent.

8 Servings

- ¾ cup all-purpose flour
- 2 tablespoons sugar
- 1 teaspoon baking powder
- ¼ teaspoon salt
- 3 tablespoons margarine
- 3 tablespoons skim milk
- 1½ cups dark sweet cherries, pitted
- 1½ cups blueberries
- 3 tablespoons sugar
- 1 tablespoon lemon juice
- 1 tablespoon lemon rind, grated
- ¼ teaspoon ground cinnamon

C ombine flour, 2 tablespoons sugar, baking powder, and salt in medium-size bowl. Cut in margarine with pastry blender or 2 knives until mixture resembles coarse crumbs. Mix in milk, stirring just enough to form a soft dough; set aside.

Combine cherries, blueberries, 3 tablespoons sugar, lemon juice, lemon rind, and cinnamon in Dutch oven or large saucepan. Heat to boiling; reduce heat and simmer, uncovered, 5 minutes.

Drop dough by rounded tablespoonfuls onto berry mixture. Cook, uncovered, 10 minutes; cover and cook an additional 10 minutes. Serve warm.

Nutritional Data

PER SERVING		EXCHANGES	
Calories:	131	Milk:	0.0
Fat (gm):	2.6	Veg.:	0.0
Cholesterol (mg):	0	Fruit:	1.5
Sodium (mg):	161	Bread:	0.5
Sat. fat (gm):	.5	Meat:	0.0
% Calories from fat:	17	Fat:	0.5

Pears Belle Hélène

Tuck a Chocolate-Glazed Cookie Crisp (see Index) beside each dish to complete this extravagant offering.

4 Servings

- 4 cups water
- ¼ cup sugar
- 4 small pears, peeled with stem intact
- 1 cup frozen low-fat vanilla yogurt
  Bittersweet Chocolate Sauce (see Index)

Combine water and sugar in small saucepan; heat to boiling. Add pears; reduce heat to low and gently simmer, covered, 10 to 15 minutes or until pears are tender.

Cool pears in syrup; refrigerate until chilled, 1 to 2 hours. Drain.

To serve, flatten a scoop of yogurt in each of 4 dessert dishes. Place a pear on top and drizzle with Chocolate Sauce.

Nutritional Data

PER SERVING		EXCHANGES	
Calories:	183	Milk:	0.0
Fat (gm):	1.1	Veg.:	0.0
Cholesterol (mg):	0	Fruit:	2.0
Sodium (mg):	0	Bread:	1.0
Sat. fat (gm):	0	Meat:	0.0
% Calories from fat:	5	Fat:	0.0

BAKED FRUIT COMPOTE WITH MERINGUE PUFFS

Spoonfuls of meringue add a creative touch to warm, baked fruits.

4 Servings

2 cups peaches, peeled, pitted, and sliced
1 pt. raspberries
¼ cup sugar
3 egg whites
3 tablespoons sugar
½ teaspoon vanilla
¼ teaspoon ground nutmeg
2 tablespoons toasted almonds, sliced

Preheat oven to 375°.

Combine peaches, raspberries, and ¼ cup sugar in medium-size bowl. Divide evenly among 4 custard cups. Place custard cups on cookie sheet and bake 10 to 15 minutes or until heated through.

Meanwhile, beat egg whites in small bowl until soft peaks form. Gradually add 3 tablespoons sugar, beating until stiff peaks form. Add vanilla and nutmeg; beat 1 minute.

Spoon meringue over warm peach mixture. Bake until lightly browned, about 10 minutes. Sprinkle with almonds and serve immediately.

Nutritional Data

PER SERVING		EXCHANGES	
Calories:	181	Milk:	0.0
Fat (gm):	2.3	Veg.:	0.0
Cholesterol (mg):	0	Fruit:	2.0
Sodium (mg):	42	Bread:	0.0
Sat. fat (gm):	.2	Meat:	1.0
% Calories from fat:	11	Fat:	0.0

TROPICAL FRUIT SOUP

If ripe mangoes are not available, the soup is still delicious made with cantaloupe or muskmelon.

8 Servings (½ cup each)

2½ cups mangoes (about 1½ lbs.), peeled, pitted, and sliced

1 can (11 ozs.) mandarin oranges, drained

1½ cups frozen low-fat vanilla yogurt

2 tablespoons lime juice

8 lime slices

In a food processor or blender, combine mangoes and oranges; blend until smooth. Add frozen yogurt and lime juice; blend until smooth. Serve in chilled soup bowls; garnish with lime slices.

Nutritional Data

PER SERVING		EXCHANGES	
Calories:	105	Milk:	0.0
Fat (gm):	.6	Veg.:	0.0
Cholesterol (mg):	0	Fruit:	1.5
Sodium (mg):	3	Bread:	0.0
Sat. fat (gm):	0	Meat:	0.0
% Calories from fat:	5	Fat:	0.0

SWEET CHERRY SOUP WITH YOGURT SWIRL

A Merlot wine would be an excellent choice for this sweet dessert soup. Serve in well-chilled bowls.

6 Servings (½ cup each)

- 2 cups frozen, slightly thawed, sweet cherries, pitted
- 1½ cups low-fat vanilla yogurt (divided)
- ¼ cup dry red wine, or cranberry juice
- 2 tablespoons lemon juice

Place cherries in food processor or blender; blend until finely chopped. Add 1 cup of yogurt, wine, and lemon juice; blend until smooth. (Texture will be frosty.) Pour into 6 chilled soup bowls. Dollop remaining yogurt onto soup; swirl with a skewer or spoon.

Nutritional Data

PER SERVING		EXCHANGES	
Calories:	178	Milk:	0.5
Fat (gm):	.7	Veg.:	0.0
Cholesterol (mg):	2	Fruit:	2.0
Sodium (mg):	37	Bread:	0.0
Sat. fat (gm):	.4	Meat:	0.0
% Calories from fat:	4	Fat:	0.0

6.
FROZEN DESSERTS

Orange-Pineapple Sherbet
Ginger-Citrus Sorbet
Lemon Ice
Pineapple-Champagne Ice
Praline Sundaes
Mixed Fruit Tortoni
Orange Baked Alaska
Chocolate Baked Alaska
Frozen Peppermint Cake Rolls

*ORANGE-PINEAPPLE SHERBET

Use an ice cream maker to produce the smoothest texture in sherbets and ices. To keep orange segments whole, add them just before freezing is completed.

8 Servings (½ cup each)

- ½ cup sugar (substitute can be used*)
- ⅓ cup water
- 1 can (15.25 ozs.) unsweetened crushed pineapple, undrained
- 1¼ cups buttermilk
- ¼ cup orange juice
- 1 can (11 ozs.) mandarin oranges, drained

Heat sugar* and water to boiling in medium-size saucepan, stirring until sugar is dissolved. Cool to room temperature.

Process pineapple, buttermilk, sugar syrup mixture and orange juice in food processor or blender until smooth. Freeze in ice cream maker according to manufacturer's directions, adding oranges just before sherbet is frozen. Or pour into 8-inch-square baking dish and freeze until slushy, about 2 hours; spoon into bowl and beat until fluffy, then stir in oranges, return to pan, and freeze until firm, 6 hours or overnight.

*Note: If using sweeteners with aspartame, mix sweetener and warm water, stirring until sweetener is dissolved; do not heat. Proceed with recipe as above.

Nutritional Data

PER SERVING			EXCHANGES	
Calories:	67	(61)	Milk:	0.0
Fat (gm):	.4		Veg.:	0.0
Cholesterol (mg):	1		Fruit:	1.0
Sodium (mg):	42		Bread:	0.0
Sat. fat (gm):	.2		Meat:	0.0
% Calories from fat:	5	(6)	Fat:	0.0

(*Changes shown in parentheses will result from substituting 8 packets Equal® for sugar.)

GINGER-CITRUS SORBET

Slightly tart, slightly zesty, very refreshing!

6 Servings

3½ cups water
1½ cups sugar
 ¼ cup gingerroot, peeled, minced
 2 teaspoons orange rind, grated
 ⅓ cup orange juice
 2 tablespoons lemon juice

Combine water, sugar, gingerroot, and orange rind in medium-size saucepan. Bring to boil over medium-high heat, stirring until sugar is dissolved; reduce heat and simmer 7 to 10 minutes. Cool to room temperature; stir in orange juice and lemon juice.

Freeze in ice cream maker according to manufacturer's directions. Or pour into 8-inch-square baking dish and freeze until slushy, 2 to 4 hours; spoon into bowl and beat until fluffy, then return to pan and freeze until firm, 6 hours.

Nutritional Data

PER SERVING		EXCHANGES	
Calories:	190	Milk:	0.0
Fat (gm):	.1	Veg.:	0.0
Cholesterol (mg):	0	Fruit:	3.0
Sodium (mg):	1	Bread:	0.0
Sat. fat (gm):	0	Meat:	0.0
% Calories from fat:	0	Fat:	0.0

LEMON ICE

Serve this sweet-and-tart ice as a dessert or as a refreshing palate cleanser between dinner courses.

8 Servings

- 2 cups water
- 1 cup sugar
- 1 cup fresh lemon juice
- ½ cup lemon rind, grated

C ombine water and sugar in medium-high saucepan. Bring to a boil over medium-high heat, stirring until sugar is dissolved. Reduce heat and simmer, uncovered, 5 minutes. Remove from heat; cool to room temperature. Stir in lemon juice and lemon rind.

Freeze in ice cream maker according to manufacturer's directions. Or pour into 8-inch-square baking dish and freeze until slushy, about 2 hours; spoon into bowl and beat until fluffy, then return to pan and freeze until firm, 6 hours or overnight.

Nutritional Data

PER SERVING		EXCHANGES	
Calories:	101	Milk:	0.0
Fat (gm):	0	Veg.:	0.0
Cholesterol (mg):	0	Fruit:	0.0
Sodium (mg):	1.3	Bread:	1.5
Sat. fat (gm):	0	Meat:	0.0
% Calories from fat:	0	Fat:	0.0

PINEAPPLE-CHAMPAGNE ICE

Champagne-inspired for a touch of elegance.

8 Servings

    1 pkg. (¼ oz.) unflavored gelatin
2½ cups unsweetened pineapple juice
  ½ cup dry champagne, or sparkling wine
  ⅛ teaspoon ground nutmeg
  8 slices fresh pineapple (½ inch thick)
     Mint Sprigs

S prinkle gelatin over pineapple juice in medium-size saucepan; let stand 2 to 3 minutes. Cook over low heat, stirring constantly, until gelatin is dissolved. Cool to room temperature. Stir in champagne and nutmeg.

Freeze in ice cream maker according to manufacturer's directions. Or pour mixture into 9-inch-square baking dish and freeze until slushy, about 2 hours; spoon into bowl and beat until fluffy, then return to pan and freeze until firm, 6 hours or overnight.

To serve, place pineapple slices on dessert plates. Top each with a scoop of Pineapple-Champagne Ice. Garnish with mint.

Nutritional Data

PER SERVING		EXCHANGES	
Calories:	66	Milk:	0.0
Fat (gm):	.1	Veg.:	0.0
Cholesterol (mg):	0	Fruit:	1.0
Sodium (mg):	2	Bread:	0.0
Sat. fat (gm):	0	Meat:	0.0
% Calories from fat:	2	Fat:	0.0

PRALINE SUNDAES

Fresh peach slices would make a flavorful addition to the sundaes, or select a sweet from the cookie chapter.

4 Servings

¼ cup packed light brown sugar
1½ teaspoons cornstarch
½ cup water
1 tablespoon bourbon or brandy (optional)
1 teaspoon margarine
½ teaspoon vanilla
2 tablespoons pecans, chopped
1 pt. frozen low-fat vanilla yogurt

Mix sugar and cornstarch in small saucepan; stir in water. Heat to boiling over medium heat, stirring constantly until thickened, about 1 minute. Stir in bourbon; cook 10 to 15 seconds. Remove from heat; stir in margarine, vanilla, and pecans. Serve warm over frozen yogurt.

Nutritional Data

PER SERVING		EXCHANGES	
Calories:	199	Milk:	0.0
Fat (gm):	3.8	Veg.:	0.0
Cholesterol (mg):	0	Fruit:	0.0
Sodium (mg):	15	Bread:	2.5
Sat. fat (gm):	.3	Meat:	0.0
% Calories from fat:	17	Fat:	0.5

Mixed Fruit Tortoni

Traditionally made with heavy cream and candied fruits, our version of this Italian favorite uses fresh seasonal fruits and low-fat topping.

12 Servings

1½ cups fresh or frozen raspberries, thawed
3 envelopes (1.3 ozs. each) low-fat whipped topping mix*
1½ cups 2% milk
½ cup sweet cherries, pitted, cut into halves (divided)
⅓ cup apricots, peeled, pitted, and cubed
⅓ cup pineapple, peeled, cored, and cubed
4 tablespoons sugar
¼ cup pistachio nuts or slivered almonds, chopped (divided)

Process raspberries in food processor or blender until smooth; strain and discard seeds.

Blend whipped topping and milk in large bowl; beat at high speed until topping forms soft peaks, about 4 minutes. Fold raspberry puree into whipped topping.

Reserve 12 cherry halves. Combine remaining cherries, apricots, and pineapple in small bowl; sprinkle with sugar and stir. Fold fruit into whipped topping mixture.

Reserve 2 tablespoons nuts. Fold remaining nuts into whipped topping mixture.

Spoon about ½ cup of mixture into 12 cupcake liners; garnish tops of each with reserved cherry halves and nuts. Place cupcake liners in muffin or baking pan; freeze until firm, 6 hours or overnight.

*Note: If desired, ½ teaspoon sherry extract can be folded into the whipped topping mixture.

Nutritional Data

PER SERVING		EXCHANGES	
Calories:	126	Milk:	0.0
Fat (gm):	3.5	Veg.:	0.0
Cholesterol (mg):	2	Fruit:	1.5
Sodium (mg):	32	Bread:	0.0
Sat. fat (gm):	.7	Meat:	0.0
% Calories from fat:	28	Fat:	0.5

ORANGE BAKED ALASKA

Create any desired flavor of frozen yogurt by substituting another liqueur for the orange. Try cherry, raspberry, or a non-fruit flavor such as almond, hazelnut, or coffee.

8 Servings

Gingersnap Crumb Crust (see Index)
- ½ cup graham cracker crumbs
- 1 tablespoon margarine
- 4 cups frozen low-fat vanilla yogurt, slightly softened
- 2 tablespoons orange-flavor liqueur, or orange juice concentrate
- ½ teaspoon ground nutmeg
- 3 egg whites
- ⅛ teaspoon cream of tartar
- ¼ cup sugar

P reheat oven to 350°. Make crumb crust, adding ½ cup graham cracker crumbs and 1 tablespoon margarine to recipe and using 8-inch pie pan.

Mix frozen yogurt, liqueur, and nutmeg; spoon into cooled pie crust. Cover with plastic wrap and freeze until firm, 8 hours or overnight.

Preheat oven to 500°. In medium-size bowl, beat egg whites with cream of tartar to soft peaks. Gradually add sugar, beating to stiff peaks. Spread meringue over frozen pie, carefully sealing to edge of crust. Bake 3 to 5 minutes or until meringue is golden. Serve immediately.

Nutritional Data

PER SERVING		EXCHANGES	
Calories:	250	Milk:	0.0
Fat (gm):	5.5	Veg.:	0.0
Cholesterol (mg):	0	Fruit:	0.0
Sodium (mg):	145	Bread:	3.0
Sat. fat (gm):	.5	Meat:	0.0
% Calories from fat:	19	Fat:	1.0

CHOCOLATE BAKED ALASKA

For an added chocolate accent, drizzle each serving with 1 to 2 teaspoons of Bittersweet Chocolate Sauce (see Index).

8 Servings

Vanilla Crumb Crust (see Index)
¼ cup vanilla wafer cookie crumbs
1 tablespoon margarine
4 cups frozen low-fat chocolate yogurt, slightly softened
3 egg whites
⅛ teaspoon cream of tartar
¼ cup sugar

Preheat oven to 350°. Make crumb crust, adding ¼ cup cookie crumbs and 1 tablespoon margarine to recipe and using 8-inch pie pan.

Spoon frozen yogurt into cooled pie crust; cover with plastic wrap and freeze until firm, 8 hours or overnight.

Preheat oven to 500°. In medium-size bowl, beat egg whites with cream of tartar to soft peaks. Gradually add sugar, beating to stiff peaks. Spread meringue over frozen pie, carefully sealing to edge of crust. Bake 3 to 5 minutes or until meringue is golden. Serve immediately.

Nutritional Data

PER SERVING		EXCHANGES	
Calories:	228	Milk:	0.0
Fat (gm):	5.5	Veg.:	0.0
Cholesterol (mg):	10	Fruit:	0.0
Sodium (mg):	108	Bread:	2.5
Sat. fat (gm):	.8	Meat:	0.0
% Calories from fat:	22	Fat:	1.0

FROZEN PEPPERMINT CAKE ROLLS

This beautiful dessert is deceptively easy to prepare, using cake mix. The cake rolls can be frozen, securely wrapped in aluminum foil, up to 1 month.

20 Servings

4 eggs
1 pkg. (18.75 ozs.) reduced-fat yellow cake mix
½ cup water
Powdered sugar
¾ cup peppermint candies, crushed
1½ qts. frozen low-fat vanilla yogurt, slightly softened
Bittersweet Chocolate Sauce (see Index)

Preheat oven to 350°. Lightly grease 2 jelly roll pans, 15 ×10 inches, and line with aluminum foil; grease foil and sprinkle with flour.

Beat eggs in medium-size bowl at high speed until thick and lemon-colored, about 5 minutes. Mix in cake mix and water on low speed.

Pour batter into prepared pans; bake 15 minutes or until cakes spring back when touched. Immediately invert cakes onto clean kitchen towels sprinkled with powdered sugar. Remove foil and roll cake up in towels, starting at short ends. Cool on wire racks 8 to 10 minutes (no longer, or cakes will be too cool to fill and roll easily).

Fold peppermint candies into yogurt. Unroll cakes; spread with candied yogurt. Roll cakes up and wrap securely in plastic wrap; freeze until firm, 8 hours or overnight. Arrange cakes on serving platters; sprinkle with powdered sugar. Cut into slices; drizzle with Chocolate Sauce.

Nutritional Data

PER SERVING		EXCHANGES	
Calories:	249	Milk:	0.0
Fat (gm):	4.4	Veg.:	0.0
Cholesterol (mg):	42.4	Fruit:	0.0
Sodium (mg):	212	Bread:	3.0
Sat. fat (gm):	1	Meat:	0.0
% Calories from fat:	16	Fat:	1.0

7.
CUSTARDS, PUDDINGS & SOUFFLES

Rich Chocolate Pudding

Old-Fashioned Baked Rice Pudding

Blueberry Bread Pudding

Warm Indian Pudding

Brown Sugar Apple Pudding

Lemon Velvet Pudding

Peach Almond Cream

Fresh Apricot Custard

Caramel Flan

Orange Flan

Chilled Raspberry Souffle

Peach-Allspice Souffles

Baked Banana Souffles

89

*RICH CHOCOLATE PUDDING

Unbelievably rich in flavor, smooth in texture. Use Dutch or European process cocoa for fullest flavor. Offer Hazelnut Meringues (see Index) as an accompaniment to this dessert.

4 Servings

- ½ cup sugar (substitute can be used*)
- ⅓ cup unsweetened cocoa
- 2 tablespoons cornstarch
- ⅛ teaspoon salt
- 2 cups 2% milk**
- 2 egg yolks, slightly beaten
- 2 teaspoons vanilla

Mix sugar,* cocoa, cornstarch, and salt in medium-size saucepan; stir in milk. Cook over medium heat until mixture boils and thickens, stirring constantly; boil 1 minute, stirring constantly.

Stir about ½ cup milk mixture into egg yolks. Stir egg yolk mixture back into saucepan. Heat to boiling over medium heat, stirring constantly; boil 1 minute (no longer!), stirring constantly. Stir in vanilla.

Spoon into dessert bowls. Refrigerate, covered with plastic wrap, until chilled, 1 to 2 hours.

*Note: If using sweeteners with aspartame, stir into pudding after it has been cooked and cooled slightly.

**Note: If using artificial sweetener, substitute skim milk.

Nutritional Data

PER SERVING			EXCHANGES		
Calories:	219	(124)	Milk:	0.5	
Fat (gm):	5.8	(3.7)	Veg.:	0.0	
Cholesterol (mg):	116	(109)	Fruit:	1.5	(1.0)
Sodium (mg):	133	(135)	Bread:	0.0	
Sat. fat (gm):	2.3	(1.0)	Meat:	0.5	(0.0)
% Calories from fat:	24	(28)	Fat:	1.0	(0.5)

(*Changes shown in parentheses will result from substituting 12 packets Equal® for sugar, and skim milk for 2% milk.)

*OLD-FASHIONED BAKED RICE PUDDING

Serve warm with Tart Lemon Sauce, Festive Cranberry Sauce, or Southern Praline Sauce (see Index).

6 Servings

½ cup uncooked converted rice

3 cups skim milk

⅓ cup sugar (substitute can be used*)

¼ cup golden raisins

½ teaspoon ground cinnamon

2 dashes ground nutmeg

P reheat oven to 300°.

Combine rice, milk, sugar,* raisins, cinnamon, and nutmeg in 2-quart casserole. Bake, uncovered, until rice is tender and milk is absorbed, about 2½ hours, stirring occasionally. Serve warm or chilled.

Note: If using sweeteners with aspartame, stir into baked pudding after it has baked and cooled 10 to 15 minutes.

Nutritional Data

PER SERVING			EXCHANGES		
Calories:	158	(124)	Milk:	0.5	
Fat (gm):	.3		Veg.:	0.0	
Cholesterol (mg):	2		Fruit:	0.5	(0.0)
Sodium (mg):	65		Bread:	1.0	
Sat. fat (gm):	.2		Meat:	0.0	
% Calories from fat:	2		Fat:	0.0	

(*Changes shown in parentheses will result from substituting 8 packets Equal® for sugar.)

*BLUEBERRY BREAD PUDDING

Add Honey Sauce, Tart Lemon Sauce, or Fresh Ginger Sauce (see Index) to complement this favorite comfort food.

8 Servings

- 6 slices whole-wheat bread
- 3 tablespoons margarine, softened
- 1 egg
- 2 egg whites
- ½ cup sugar (substitute can be used, but not aspartame*)
- ¼ teaspoon salt
- 2 cups skim milk
- 1 teaspoon vanilla
- 1 cup fresh or frozen blueberries

Preheat oven to 350°. Lightly grease 9-inch baking dish.

Spread margarine on one side of each slice of bread; cut into 2-inch squares and place in prepared dish.

Combine egg, egg whites, sugar,* and salt in medium-size bowl. Meanwhile, heat milk in small saucepan until just boiling; stir milk into egg mixture. Stir in vanilla and blueberries; pour over bread cubes.

Place baking dish in a 10×15-inch roasting pan; pour 1 inch hot water into pan. Bake 35 to 40 minutes or until knife inserted near center comes out clean. Serve warm or room temperature.

Nutritional Data

PER SERVING			EXCHANGES	
Calories:	162	(123)	Milk:	0.0
Fat (gm):	3.9		Veg.:	0.0
Cholesterol (mg):	28		Fruit:	1.0 (0.5)
Sodium (mg):	303	(309)	Bread:	1.0
Sat. fat (gm):	.6		Meat:	0.0
% Calories from fat:	21	(28)	Fat:	0.5

(*Changes shown in parentheses will result from substituting 12 packets Sweet 'n Low® for sugar.)

WARM INDIAN PUDDING

Molasses and sweet spices signal the welcome flavors of the fall season.

6 Servings

¼ cup yellow cornmeal
2¾ cups skim milk
¾ cup light molasses
⅓ cup packed light brown sugar
¼ teaspoon salt
3 tablespoons margarine
¼ cup dark raisins
½ teaspoon ground cinnamon
¼ teaspoon ground nutmeg
⅛ teaspoon ground cloves
⅛ teaspoon ground ginger
¼ cup skim milk

 Preheat oven to 325°.

Combine cornmeal and 1 cup of the milk in a small bowl; set aside.

Heat remaining 1¾ cups of the milk in a medium-size saucepan until steaming. Stir in cornmeal mixture and cook until thickened, 15 minutes, stirring occasionally. Stir in molasses, sugar, and salt. Cook 2 to 3 minutes to dissolve sugar. Remove from heat; stir in margarine, raisins, cinnamon, nutmeg, cloves, and ginger.

Spoon mixture into greased 1½-quart casserole. Pour ¼ cup milk over mixture; bake, uncovered, 1¼ hours or until knife inserted near center comes out clean. Serve warm.

Nutritional Data

PER SERVING		EXCHANGES	
Calories:	250	Milk:	0.5
Fat (gm):	3.3	Veg.:	0.0
Cholesterol (mg):	2	Fruit:	3.0
Sodium (mg):	229	Bread:	0.0
Sat. fat (gm):	.7	Meat:	0.0
% Calories from fat:	11	Fat:	0.5

BROWN SUGAR APPLE PUDDING

Topped and baked with a batter and brown sugar syrup, this is the best apple pudding you will ever eat!

10 Servings

Pudding

  8 cups apples, peeled, cored, sliced (¼-in. slices)
  ½ cup packed light brown sugar
  ¼ cup margarine, softened
1½ teaspoons ground cinnamon
  1 egg
  ½ teaspoon vanilla
  ¾ cup all-purpose flour
  2 teaspoons baking powder
  ¼ teaspoon salt
  ½ cup skim milk

Brown Sugar Syrup

  ½ cup packed light brown sugar
  2 tablespoons flour
  1 teaspoon margarine
  1 cup water
  ½ teaspoon vanilla

Pudding: Preheat oven to 375°. Lightly grease 1-quart casserole with cooking spray; arrange apple slices in casserole and set aside.

Combine brown sugar, margarine, and cinnamon in medium-size bowl until smooth. Stir in egg and vanilla.

Combine flour, baking powder, and salt in small bowl and add to egg mixture alternately with milk, stirring only until blended.

Spread batter over apple slices.

Brown Sugar Syrup: Combine brown sugar, flour, and margarine in small saucepan. Stir in water and heat to boiling, stirring constantly. Boil 2 to 3 minutes, stirring constantly. Remove from heat and stir in vanilla. Pour Brown Sugar Syrup over batter. Bake, uncovered, 50 to 55 minutes or until apples are tender. Serve warm or at room temperature.

Nutritional Data

PER SERVING		EXCHANGES	
Calories:	213	Milk:	0.0
Fat (gm):	3.7	Veg.:	0.0
Cholesterol (mg):	21.5	Fruit:	2.0
Sodium (mg):	203	Bread:	1.0
Sat. fat (gm):	.7	Meat:	0.0
% Calories from fat:	16	Fat:	0.5

*LEMON VELVET PUDDING

Top this velvet-textured custard with fresh peaches, strawberries, or other seasonal fruit. Serve a plate of Apricot-Sesame Biscotti (see Index) on the side.

4 Servings

½ cup sugar (substitute can be used*)
2 tablespoons cornstarch**
⅛ teaspoon salt
2 cups 2% milk**
2 egg yolks, slightly beaten
2 tablespoons lemon juice
1 teaspoon lemon extract

Mix sugar,* cornstarch, and salt in medium-size saucepan; stir in milk. Cook over medium heat until mixture boils and thickens, stirring constantly; boil 1 minute, stirring constantly.

Stir about ½ cup milk mixture into egg yolks. Stir egg yolk mixture back into saucepan; stir in lemon juice and extract. Heat to boiling over medium heat, stirring constantly; boil 1 minute (no longer!), stirring constantly.

Spoon into dessert dishes. Refrigerate, covered with plastic wrap, until chilled, 1 to 2 hours.

*Note: If using sweeteners with aspartame, stir into pudding after it has been cooked and cooled slightly.

**Note : If using artificial sweetener, use 3 tablespoons cornstarch and substitute skim milk.

Nutritional Data

PER SERVING			EXCHANGES		
Calories:	201	(105)	Milk:	0.5	
Fat (gm):	4.9	(2.8)	Veg.:	0.0	
Cholesterol (mg):	116	(109)	Fruit:	1.5	(0.5)
Sodium (mg):	132	(134)	Bread:	0.0	
Sat. fat (gm):	2.2	(1.0)	Meat:	0.5	(0.0)
% Calories from fat:	22	(24)	Fat:	1.0	(0.5)

(*Changes shown in parentheses will result from substituting 12 packets Equal® for sugar, and skim milk for 2% milk.)

*PEACH ALMOND CREAM

This shimmery, delicate gelatin custard is reminiscent of the oriental dessert often made with mandarin oranges and lychee fruit.

6 Servings

2 envelopes unflavored gelatin
⅓ cup sugar (substitute can be used*)
1 qt. 2% milk
½ teaspoon almond extract
1 cup sliced peaches packed in juice, drained

S prinkle gelatin and sugar* over milk in medium-size saucepan; let stand 2 to 3 minutes. Cook over medium-low heat, stirring constantly, until gelatin is dissolved. Stir in almond extract.

Pour mixture into medium-size bowl; refrigerate until mixture is consistency of unbeaten egg whites, about 1 hour. Stir in peaches; spoon into individual dishes. Refrigerate until custard is set, 2 to 3 hours.

*Note: If using sweeteners with aspartame, stir into custard after it has been cooked and cooled slightly.

Nutritional Data

PER SERVING			EXCHANGES		
Calories:	140	(106)	Milk:	1.0	
Fat (gm):	3.2		Veg.:	0.0	
Cholesterol (mg):	12		Fruit:	0.5	(0.0)
Sodium (mg):	86		Bread:	0.0	
Sat. fat (gm):	1.9		Meat:	0.0	
% Calories from fat:	20	(27)	Fat:	0.5	

(*Changes shown in parentheses will result from substituting 8 packets Equal® for sugar.)

*FRESH APRICOT CUSTARD

A delicate custard with fresh apricots gently folded throughout. Serve with cookies—Gingersnappers (see Index) would be nice.

6 Servings

- ½ cup sugar (substitute can be used*)
- 3 tablespoons cornstarch
- 2 cups skim milk
- ½ cup apricot nectar
- 2 egg yolks, slightly beaten
- 2 tablespoons margarine
- 1½ cups fresh apricots (7 medium apricots), peeled, coarsely chopped

Mix sugar* and cornstarch in medium-size saucepan; stir in milk and apricot nectar. Cook over medium heat until mixture boils and thickens, stirring constantly; boil 1 minute, stirring constantly.

Stir about ½ cup milk mixture into egg yolks; stir egg yolk mixture back into saucepan. Heat to boiling over medium heat, stirring constantly; boil 1 minute (no longer!), stirring constantly.

Remove from heat; stir in margarine. Refrigerate, covered with plastic wrap, until chilled, 1 to 2 hours.

Stir custard until fluffy; stir in apricots. Spoon into dessert dishes.

*Note: If using sweeteners with aspartame, stir into custard after it has been cooked and cooled.

Nutritional Data

PER SERVING			EXCHANGES		
Calories:	168	(116)	Milk:	0.5	
Fat (gm):	3.9		Veg.:	0.0	
Cholesterol (mg):	72		Fruit:	1.5	(0.5)
Sodium (mg):	91		Bread:	0.0	
Sat. fat (gm):	1		Meat:	0.0	
% Calories from fat:	20	(29)	Fat:	1.0	

(*Changes shown in parentheses will result from substituting 12 packets Equal® for sugar.)

CARAMEL FLAN

Unbelievably delicate and fine in texture, this flan is one you'll serve over and over again.

8 Servings

¼ cup sugar
4 cups skim milk
⅓ cup sugar
5 eggs
2 teaspoons vanilla

Heat ¼ cup sugar in small skillet over medium-high heat until sugar melts and turns golden, stirring occasionally (watch carefully—the sugar can burn easily!). Quickly pour syrup into bottom of 2-quart souffle or casserole and tilt bottom to spread caramel. Set aside to cool.

Preheat oven to 350°.

Heat milk and ⅓ cup sugar until steaming and just beginning to bubble at edges. Beat eggs in medium-size bowl; stir in hot milk and vanilla.

Pour mixture through strainer into souffle dish. Place souffle dish in roasting pan on middle oven rack. Cover souffle dish with lid or aluminum foil. Pour 2 inches hot water into roasting pan.

Bake 1 hour or until sharp knife inserted halfway between center and edge of custard comes out clean. Remove souffle dish from roasting pan and cool to room temperature on wire rack. Refrigerate 8 hours or overnight.

To unmold, loosen edge of custard with sharp knife. Place rimmed serving dish over souffle dish and invert.

Nutritional Data

PER SERVING		EXCHANGES	
Calories:	146	Milk:	0.5
Fat (gm):	3.4	Veg.:	0.0
Cholesterol (mg):	135	Fruit:	1.0
Sodium (mg):	103	Bread:	0.0
Sat. fat (gm):	1.1	Meat:	0.5
% Calories from fat:	21	Fat:	0.5

ORANGE FLAN

This flan is scented with orange for a subtle flavor accent.

8 Servings

¼ cup sugar
3¾ cups skim milk
¼ cup frozen orange juice concentrate
⅓ cup sugar
6 eggs
⅛ teaspoon orange extract

Heat ¼ cup sugar in small skillet over medium-high heat until sugar melts and turns golden, stirring occasionally (watch carefully—the sugar can burn easily!). Quickly pour syrup into bottom of 2-quart souffle or casserole and tilt bottom to spread caramel. Set aside to cool.

Preheat oven to 350°.

Heat milk, orange juice concentrate, and ⅓ cup sugar in medium-size saucepan until steaming and just beginning to bubble at edges. Beat eggs in medium-size bowl; stir in hot milk mixture and orange extract.

Pour mixture through strainer into souffle dish. Place souffle dish in roasting pan on middle oven rack. Cover souffle dish with lid or aluminum foil. Pour 2 inches hot water into roasting pan.

Bake 1 hour or until sharp knife inserted halfway between center and edge of custard comes out clean. Remove souffle dish from roasting pan and cool to room temperature on wire rack. Refrigerate 8 hours or overnight.

To unmold, loosen edge of custard with sharp knife. Place rimmed serving dish over souffle dish and invert.

Nutritional Data

PER SERVING		EXCHANGES	
Calories:	161	Milk:	0.5
Fat (gm):	4.0	Veg.:	0.0
Cholesterol (mg):	162	Fruit:	1.0
Sodium (mg):	107	Bread:	0.0
Sat. fat (gm):	1.3	Meat:	1.0
% Calories from fat:	22	Fat:	0.5

CHILLED RASPBERRY SOUFFLE

Serve this delicate souffle with Summer Raspberry Coulis (see Index).

6 Servings (½ cup each)

⅓ cup sugar
½ cup water
3 teaspoons lemon juice
1 package (¼ oz.) unflavored gelatin
2 cups fresh or frozen, thawed, raspberries
2 envelopes (1.3 ozs. each) low-fat whipped
  topping mix
1 cup 2% milk
  Fresh raspberries (optional)
  Mint sprigs (optional)

C ombine sugar, water, and lemon juice in small saucepan;
sprinkle in gelatin. Let stand 2 to 3 minutes. Bring to a simmer
over medium heat, stirring constantly until sugar and gelatin are
dissolved. Cool until mixture is consistency of unbeaten egg whites.

Process 2 cups raspberries in food processor or blender until smooth;
strain and discard seeds. Blend whipped topping and milk in large bowl;
beat at high speed until topping forms soft peaks, about 4 minutes. Stir
raspberry puree into gelatin mixture; fold in whipped topping.

Spoon into serving dish or individual stemmed dishes. Chill 2 to 4
hours or until set. Garnish with fresh raspberries and mint.

Nutritional Data

PER SERVING		EXCHANGES	
Calories:	69	Milk:	0.0
Fat (gm):	1	Veg.:	0.0
Cholesterol (mg):	3	Fruit:	1.5
Sodium (mg):	30	Bread:	0.0
Sat. fat (gm):	.5	Meat:	0.0
% Calories from fat:	14	Fat:	1.0

PEACH-ALLSPICE SOUFFLES

6 Servings

Vegetable cooking spray
1½ cups fresh peaches, peeled, diced (well-drained frozen and thawed or canned peaches may be substituted)
2 teaspoons lemon juice
1 teaspoon vanilla
1 teaspoon sugar
⅛ teaspoon ground allspice
2 egg yolks
4 egg whites
⅛ teaspoon cream of tartar
¼ cup sugar
Powdered sugar

reheat oven to 450°. Spray six 1-cup souffle dishes* or custard cups with cooking spray; place dishes on baking sheet and set aside.

Process peaches, lemon juice, vanilla, 1 teaspoon sugar, and allspice in food processor or blender until smooth. Add egg yolks, one at a time, scraping sides of container occasionally; transfer mixture to a bowl and set aside.

In medium-size bowl, beat egg whites with cream of tartar until soft peaks form. Gradually beat in ¼ cup sugar, beating to stiff peaks. Fold in peach mixture. Spoon into prepared dishes.

Bake 7 minutes; reduce heat to 425° and bake 7 minutes more or until souffles are lightly browned and sharp knife inserted near centers comes out clean. Remove from oven, sprinkle with powdered sugar, and serve immediately.

*Note: Souffle can be baked in a 1-quart souffle dish. Bake at 450° for 10 minutes; reduce heat to 425° and bake 10 minutes more or until sharp knife inserted near center comes out clean.

Nutritional Data

PER SERVING		EXCHANGES	
Calories:	85	Milk:	0.0
Fat (gm):	1.7	Veg.:	0.0
Cholesterol (mg):	71	Fruit:	1.0
Sodium (mg):	39	Bread:	0.0
Sat. fat (gm):	.5	Meat:	0.5
% Calories from fat:	18	Fat:	0.0

BAKED BANANA SOUFFLES

For perfect flavor and texture, select bananas that are ripe and soft, but not overripe.

6 Servings

Vegetable cooking spray
2 ripe medium bananas, peeled
2 teaspoons lemon juice
1 teaspoon vanilla
1 teaspoon sugar
¼ teaspoon ground nutmeg
2 egg yolks
4 egg whites
⅛ teaspoon cream of tartar
3 tablespoons sugar
Powdered sugar

 reheat oven to 450°. Spray six 1-cup souffle dishes* or custard cups with cooking spray; place dishes on baking sheet and set aside.

Process bananas, lemon juice, vanilla, 1 teaspoon sugar, and nutmeg in food processor or blender until smooth. Add egg yolks, one at a time, scraping sides of container occasionally; transfer mixture to a bowl.

In medium-size bowl, beat egg whites with cream of tartar until soft peaks form. Gradually beat in 3 tablespoons sugar, beating to stiff peaks. Fold in banana mixture. Spoon into prepared dishes.

Bake 7 minutes; reduce heat to 425° and bake 7 minutes more or until souffles are lightly browned and sharp knife inserted near centers comes out clean. Remove from oven, sprinkle with powdered sugar, and serve immediately.

*Note: Souffle can be baked in a 1-quart souffle dish. Bake at 450° for 10 minutes; reduce heat to 425° and bake 10 minutes more or until sharp knife inserted near center comes out clean.

Nutritional Data

PER SERVING		EXCHANGES	
Calories:	94	Milk:	0.0
Fat (gm):	1.9	Veg.:	0.0
Cholesterol (mg):	71	Fruit:	1.0
Sodium (mg):	39	Bread:	0.0
Sat. fat (gm):	.6	Meat:	0.5
% Calories from fat:	18	Fat:	0.0

8.
DESSERT SAUCES

Summer Raspberry Coulis

Pineapple-Rum Sauce

Tart Lemon Sauce

Brandied Cherry Sauce

Festive Cranberry Sauce

Orange Marmalade Sauce

Honey Sauce

Warm Rum Sauce

Bittersweet Chocolate Sauce

Berries 'n Cream Sauce

Herb-Scented Citrus Cream

105

*SUMMER RASPBERRY COULIS

Entertain with flair, adding this fresh berry coulis to Apricot and Peach Fillo Nests or Kiwi Cream Tart (see Index).

8 Servings (2 tablespoons each)

1 pt. fresh or frozen, thawed, raspberries
¼ cup sugar (substitute can be used*)
1 teaspoon lemon juice

 n a blender or food processor, combine raspberries, sugar,* and lemon juice. Puree until smooth. Strain the puree; discard seeds.

Nutritional Data

PER SERVING			EXCHANGES	
Calories:	38	(18)	Milk:	0.0
Fat (gm):	.2		Veg.:	0.0
Cholesterol (mg):	0		Fruit:	0.5 (0.0)
Sodium (mg):	0		Bread:	0.0
Sat. fat (gm):	0		Meat:	0.0
% Calories from fat:	4	(8)	Fat:	0.0

(*Changes shown in parentheses will result from substituting 6 packets Equal® for sugar.)

*Pineapple-Rum Sauce

A perfect complement to Streusel-Topped Carrot Cake, New York-Style Cheesecake (see Index), or low-fat frozen yogurt.

12 Servings (2 tablespoons each)

1½ cups unsweetened pineapple-orange juice
1 cup pineapple, pared, cored, coarsely chopped
¼ cup sugar (substitute can be used*)
1 tablespoon rum, or ½-1 teaspoon rum extract
2 teaspoons cornstarch
⅛-¼ teaspoon ground nutmeg

Mix juice, pineapple, sugar,* rum, and cornstarch in small saucepan; heat to boiling. Cook, stirring constantly, until thickened; boil 1 minute, stirring constantly. Remove from heat and stir in nutmeg. Serve warm or cold.

*Note: If using sweeteners with aspartame, stir into sauce after it has been cooked and cooled slightly.

Nutritional Data

PER SERVING			EXCHANGES	
Calories:	37	(24)	Milk:	0.0
Fat (gm):	0		Veg.:	0.0
Cholesterol (mg):	0		Fruit:	0.5
Sodium (mg):	1	(0)	Bread:	0.0
Sat. fat (gm):	0		Meat:	0.0
% Calories from fat:	9	(2)	Fat:	0.0

(*Changes shown in parentheses will result from substituting 6 packets Equal® for sugar.)

*TART LEMON SAUCE

Blueberry Bread Pudding and Pumpkin Ginger Cakes (see Index) are perfect choices for this nicely tart sauce.

6 Servings (2 tablespoons each)

1 tablespoon margarine**
⅓-½ cup sugar (substitute can be used*)
½ cup lemon juice
1 egg, slightly beaten

Melt margarine over low heat in small saucepan; stir in sugar* and lemon juice. Cook over medium heat until sugar is dissolved.

Gradually blend about ¼ cup of hot lemon mixture into egg. Return egg mixture to saucepan.

Cook over low heat until thickened, 2 to 3 minutes, stirring constantly. Serve warm or room temperature.

*Note: If using sweeteners with aspartame, stir into sauce after it has been cooked and cooled slightly.

**Note: If using artificial sweetener, omit margarine.

Nutritional Data

PER SERVING			EXCHANGES	
Calories:	93	(34)	Milk:	0.0
Fat (gm):	1.6	(1.8)	Veg.:	0.0
Cholesterol (mg):	32	(35)	Fruit:	0.0
Sodium (mg):	29	(32)	Bread:	1.0 (0.5)
Sat. fat (gm):	.3	(.4)	Meat:	0.0
% Calories from fat:	17	(45)	Fat:	0.0

(*Changes shown in parentheses will result from substituting 12 packets Equal® for sugar.)

*BRANDIED CHERRY SAUCE

Accent New York-Style Cheesecake or Chocolate Baked Alaska (see Index) with this flavorful sauce.

8 Servings (2 tablespoons each)

2 tablespoons sugar (substitute can be used*)
1 teaspoon cornstarch
⅛-¼ teaspoon ground allspice
1 cup fresh or frozen, thawed, pitted dark sweet cherries
½ cup water
1 tablespoon brandy, or ¼-½ teaspoon brandy extract
1 tablespoon lemon juice

Mix sugar,* cornstarch, and allspice in medium-size skillet or chafing dish. Stir in cherries, water, brandy, and lemon juice. Cook over medium heat until mixture boils and thickens, stirring constantly; boil 1 minute, stirring constantly. Serve warm.

*Note: If using sweeteners with aspartame, stir into sauce after it has been cooked and cooled slightly.

Nutritional Data

PER SERVING			EXCHANGES	
Calories:	27	(17)	Milk:	0.0
Fat (gm):	.1		Veg.:	0.0
Cholesterol (mg):	0		Fruit:	0.0
Sodium (mg):	1		Bread:	0.5 (0.0)
Sat. fat (gm):	0		Meat:	0.0
% Calories from fat:	2	(3)	Fat:	0.0

(*Changes shown in parentheses will result from substituting Equal® for sugar.)

*FESTIVE CRANBERRY SAUCE

Add holiday spirit and Festive Cranberry Sauce to New York-Style Cheesecake, Rich Lemon Pound Cake, (see Index), or baked apples. Cheers!

12 Servings (2 tablespoons each)

½ cup sugar (substitute can be used*)
1 tablespoon cornstarch
¼ teaspoon ground cinnamon
1 cup water
½ cup fresh or frozen, thawed, cranberries

C ombine sugar,* cornstarch, and cinnamon in small saucepan. Stir in water and cranberries; heat to boiling. Cook, stirring constantly, until thickened. Serve warm or cold.

*Note: If using sweeteners with aspartame, stir into sauce after it has been cooked and cooled slightly.

Nutritional Data

PER SERVING			EXCHANGES	
Calories:	35	(9)	Milk:	0.0
Fat (gm):	0		Veg.:	0.0
Cholesterol (mg):	0		Fruit:	0.5 (0.0)
Sodium (mg):	0		Bread:	0.0
Sat. fat (gm):	0		Meat:	0.0
% Calories from fat:	0	(1)	Fat:	0.0

(*Changes shown in parentheses will result from substituting Equal® for sugar.)

ORANGE MARMALADE SAUCE

Serve over Orange-Poppy Seed Cake or Rich Lemon Pound Cake (see Index) for rave reviews. Old-Fashioned Baked Rice Pudding (see Index) is another choice for this flavorful sauce.

12 Servings (2 tablespoons each)

¾ cup orange marmalade spreadable fruit
2 teaspoons cornstarch
⅔ cup cold water
2 teaspoons orange juice

H eat marmalade to boiling in small saucepan over medium heat. Mix cornstarch and water until smooth; stir into marmalade. Cook, stirring constantly, until thickened; boil 1 minute, stirring constantly. Remove from heat and stir in orange juice. Serve warm or cold.

Nutritional Data

PER SERVING		EXCHANGES	
Calories:	28	Milk:	0.0
Fat (gm):	0	Veg.:	0.0
Cholesterol (mg):	0	Fruit:	0.0
Sodium (mg):	18	Bread:	0.0
Sat. fat (gm):	0	Meat:	0.0
% Calories from fat:	0	Fat:	0.0

Honey Sauce

Serve warm or room temperature over low-fat frozen vanilla yogurt, Pumpkin Ginger Cake (see Index), or fresh fruit.

8 Servings

½ cup honey
½ cup apple juice
1 tablespoon cornstarch
2 tablespoons cold water
1 tablespoon margarine
2 teaspoons lemon juice
⅛ teaspoon ground mace

Heat honey and apple juice to boiling in small saucepan over medium heat. Mix cornstarch in cold water until smooth; stir into honey. Cook, stirring constantly, until thickened. Stir in margarine, lemon juice, and mace. Serve warm or room temperature.

Nutritional Data

PER SERVING		EXCHANGES	
Calories:	82	Milk:	0.0
Fat (gm):	.7	Veg.:	0.0
Cholesterol (mg):	0	Fruit:	1.5
Sodium (mg):	18	Bread:	0.0
Sat. fat (gm):	.1	Meat:	0.0
% Calories from fat:	8	Fat:	0.0

*Warm Rum Sauce

Delicious spooned over Old-Fashioned Baked Rice Pudding or Pumpkin Ginger Cake (see Index).

---

12 Servings (2 tablespoons each)

¼ cup sugar (substitute can be used*)
1 tablespoon cornstarch
1¼ cups skim milk
2 tablespoons rum or ½ teaspoon rum extract
2 tablespoons margarine**
½ teaspoon vanilla
⅛ teaspoon ground nutmeg

Mix sugar* and cornstarch in small saucepan; stir in milk and rum. Cook over medium heat until mixture boils and thickens, stirring constantly. Remove from heat; stir in margarine, vanilla, and nutmeg. Serve warm.

*Note: If using sweeteners with aspartame, stir into sauce after it has been cooked and cooled.

**Note: If using artificial sweetener, use only 1 tablespoon margarine.

Nutritional Data

PER SERVING			EXCHANGES		
Calories:	41	(28)	Milk:	0.5	(0.0)
Fat (gm):	1		Veg.:	0.0	
Cholesterol (mg):	0		Fruit:	0.0	
Sodium (mg):	35		Bread:	0.0	
Sat. fat (gm):	.2		Meat:	0.0	
% Calories from fat:	22	(33)	Fat:	0.0	(0.5)

(*Changes shown in parentheses will result from substituting Equal® for sugar.)

BITTERSWEET CHOCOLATE SAUCE

Bittersweet and scrumptious—serve over low-fat frozen yogurt, Chocolate Baked Alaska, or Frozen Peppermint Cake Rolls (see Index).

12 Servings (2 tablespoons each)

¾ cup unsweetened cocoa
½ cup sugar
¾ cup skim milk
2 tablespoons margarine
1 teaspoon vanilla
¼-½ teaspoon ground cinnamon

Mix cocoa and sugar in small saucepan; stir in milk and add margarine. Heat over medium heat until boiling, stirring constantly. Reduce heat and simmer until sauce is smooth and slightly thickened. Remove from heat; stir in vanilla and cinnamon. Serve warm or room temperature.

Nutritional Data

PER SERVING		EXCHANGES	
Calories:	57	Milk:	0.0
Fat (gm):	1.6	Veg.:	0.0
Cholesterol (mg):	0	Fruit:	0.0
Sodium (mg):	30	Bread:	1.0
Sat. fat (gm):	.2	Meat:	0.0
% Calories from fat:	26	Fat:	0.0

*BERRIES 'N CREAM SAUCE

First-prize honors will be awarded when this sauce is served with fresh fruit or Rich Lemon Pound Cake (see Index). Also try it with pancakes or waffles for brunch!

8 Servings (2 tablespoons each)

1 cup fresh or frozen, thawed, unsweetened raspberries
3 tablespoons sugar (substitute can be used*)
3 tablespoons non-fat sour cream
2 tablespoons lemon juice

rocess raspberries and sugar* in food processor or blender until smooth. Strain and discard seeds. Stir in sour cream and lemon juice.

Nutritional Data

PER SERVING			EXCHANGES		
Calories:	26	(20)	Milk:	0.0	
Fat (gm):	.1	(1)	Veg.:	0.0	
Cholesterol (mg):	0		Fruit:	0.0	
Sodium (mg):	6		Bread:	0.5	(0.0)
Sat. fat (gm):	0	(.7)	Meat:	0.0	
% Calories from fat:	3	(41)	Fat:	0.0	(0.5)

(*Changes shown in parentheses will result from substituting 4½ packets Equal® for sugar.)

Herb-Scented Citrus Cream

Cilantro adds a fresh sparkle of flavor to this refreshing sauce; fresh mint would be a delicious variation. Serve over Angel Food Cake (see Index), sliced fresh fruit, or Mixed Fruit Kabobs (see Index).

8 Servings (2 tablespoons each)

½ cup non-fat sour cream
½ cup low-fat custard-style lemon yogurt
1 tablespoon sugar
2 tablespoons fresh cilantro, minced
1 tablespoon orange rind, grated

C ombine sour cream, yogurt, and sugar in small bowl until smooth. Stir in cilantro and orange rind. Refrigerate 1 to 2 hours for flavors to blend.

Nutritional Data

PER SERVING		EXCHANGES	
Calories:	36	Milk:	0.0
Fat (gm):	.2	Veg.:	0.0
Cholesterol (mg):	0	Fruit:	0.0
Sodium (mg):	10	Bread:	0.0
Sat. fat (gm):	0	Meat:	0.0
% Calories from fat:	6	Fat:	0.0

9.
GOURMET ENDINGS

Buñuelos with Fruit Salsa

Strawberries with Peppercorns

Baked Fruit Compotes

Apricot and Peach Fillo Nests

Rustic Country Fruit Tart

Cassata Siciliana

Herbed Custard Brûlée

Fresh Fruit with Roquefort Sherbet

Chocolate Yogurt Cheese with Fruit

Minted Goat's Cheese with Blueberries

Fresh Ginger Sauce

Crème Anglaise

*Buñuelos with Fruit Salsa

Often served at holiday time in Mexico, these buñuelos are perfect any time of year. Top each with a small scoop of low-fat strawberry or low-fat vanilla frozen yogurt.

---

6 Servings

3 tablespoons sugar (substitute can be used*)
¼ teaspoon ground cinnamon
6 flour or whole-wheat tortillas
  Vegetable cooking spray
1 cup pineapple, peeled, cubed
1 cup mango, peeled, seeded, sliced
1 cup strawberries, halved
½ teaspoon jalapeño pepper, minced
¼ cup sugar (substitute can be used*)

reheat oven to 350°.

Combine 3 tablespoons sugar* and cinnamon in small bowl.

Lightly spray 1 side of each tortilla with cooking spray; sprinkle with cinnamon-sugar mixture. Bake on cookie sheet 5 to 8 minutes or until lightly browned and crisp.

Mix pineapple, mango, strawberries, jalapeño pepper, and ¼ cup sugar. Spoon onto warm tortillas and serve.

*Note: If using sweeteners with aspartame, sprinkle cinnamon mixture onto tortillas after they have been baked and cooled slightly.

Nutritional Data

PER SERVING			EXCHANGES		
Calories:	190	(145)	Milk:	0.0	
Fat (gm):	2.1		Veg.:	0.0	
Cholesterol (mg):	0		Fruit:	0.0	(1.0)
Sodium (mg):	1		Bread:	0.0	(1.0)
Sat. fat (gm):	0		Meat:	0.0	
% Calories from fat:	9	(13)	Fat:	0.0	(0.5)

(*Changes shown in parentheses will result from substituting 10½ packets Equal® for sugar.)

STRAWBERRIES WITH PEPPERCORNS

An unusual combination of flavors create a superb berry dessert.

6 Servings

- 1 qt. strawberries
- 2 tablespoons raspberry vinegar
- ½ teaspoon lime juice
- 2 teaspoons sugar
- 1-2 tablespoons green peppercorns, drained

Cut strawberries into halves (or quarters if they are large); spoon into serving bowl.

Combine vinegar, lime juice, and sugar in small bowl; stir in peppercorns. Sprinkle over berries and toss. Refrigerate 1 hour for flavors to blend.

Nutritional Data

PER SERVING		EXCHANGES	
Calories:	35	Milk:	0.0
Fat (gm):	.4	Veg.:	0.0
Cholesterol (mg):	0	Fruit:	0.5
Sodium (mg):	1	Bread:	0.0
Sat. fat (gm):	0	Meat:	0.0
% Calories from fat:	8	Fat:	0.0

BAKED FRUIT COMPOTES IN PARCHMENT

An impressive presentation, an elegant dessert.

8 Servings

- 2 cups apples, peeled, cored, sliced
- 1½ cups pears, peeled, cored, sliced
- 1 cup raspberries
- 3 tablespoons brown sugar
- 1 teaspoon ground cinnamon
- ¼ teaspoon ground nutmeg
- 3 teaspoons flour
- 3 tablespoons margarine, melted

Preheat oven to 375°.

Combine all ingredients, except margarine, in large bowl; gently toss.

Cut 8 (12-inch) squares of parchment paper; fold in half diagonally, making a triangle. Place triangles on baking sheets and open out flat; brush with margarine. Evenly divide fruit mixture on papers and fold in half; fold edges inward twice to seal. Bake 10 minutes.

Place packets on plates. To open, cut a 2-inch "X" in top of each packet with sharp knife.

Nutritional Data

PER SERVING		EXCHANGES	
Calories:	79	Milk:	0.0
Fat (gm):	2.3	Veg.:	0.0
Cholesterol (mg):	0	Fruit:	1.0
Sodium (mg):	51	Bread:	0.0
Sat. fat (gm):	.4	Meat:	0.0
% Calories from fat:	25	Fat:	0.5

APRICOT AND PEACH FILLO NESTS

A beautiful dessert that is quite easy to prepare; serve with Summer Raspberry Coulis (see Index).

6 Servings

- 12 sheets frozen, thawed, fillo pastry
  Butter-flavor vegetable cooking spray
- 1½ lbs. apricots, peeled, pitted, sliced
- ¾ lb. peaches, peeled, pitted, sliced
- 3 tablespoons packed light brown sugar
- ½ teaspoon ground cinnamon
- ¼ teaspoon ground nutmeg
  Mint sprigs

Preheat oven to 375°.

Cut fillo into 8-inch squares (24). Spray 4 squares of fillo lightly with vegetable spray; layer squares, turning each slightly so that corners are staggered. Carefully fit fillo into 8-ounce custard cup, shaping edges to form "nest." Repeat with remaining fillo squares lining a total of 6 custard cups. Arrange fruit in bottom of each "nest."

Combine brown sugar, cinnamon, and nutmeg; sprinkle evenly over fruit.

Place custard cups on cookie sheet and bake until fillo is golden and fruit tender, about 15 minutes. Cool on wire rack; carefully remove "nests" from custard cups. Serve warm or room temperature garnished with mint.

Nutritional Data

PER SERVING		EXCHANGES	
Calories:	185	Milk:	0.0
Fat (gm):	.9	Veg.:	0.0
Cholesterol (mg):	0	Fruit:	2.0
Sodium (mg):	4	Bread:	1.0
Sat. fat (gm):	0	Meat:	0.0
% Calories from fat:	4	Fat:	0.0

RUSTIC COUNTRY FRUIT TART

Perfect for a lazy-day summer picnic—a tumble of garden fruits, lightly glazed and encased in a free-form pastry.

8 Servings

Basic Pie Crust (All-Purpose Flour, see Index)
- ¼ cup all-purpose flour
- 2 tablespoons cold margarine
- 1 pt. raspberries
- 1 pt. strawberries, sliced
- 1 cup seedless grapes
- 3 medium apricots, pitted, cut in half
- 3 medium peaches or nectarines, peeled, pitted, cut in half
- ¼ cup all-purpose flour
- ⅓ cup sugar
- ½ teaspoon ground cinnamon
- ¼ cup apricot spreadable fruit
- 2 tablespoons water

Preheat oven to 425°. Prepare pie crust, adding ¼ cup flour and 2 tablespoons margarine to recipe. Roll pastry on lightly floured surface into a 12-inch circle. (Edges do not need to be even.) Transfer pastry to a 12-inch pizza pan.

Toss fruits with combined ¼ cup flour, sugar, and cinnamon. Arrange fruits in center of pastry, leaving a 2- to 3-inch border around outer edge. Gently gather and fold outer edge of pastry over fruits. (Fruits will not be completely enclosed. Tart should have a rustic look.)

Bake 20 to 25 minutes or until crust is lightly browned and fruit is tender. Cut into wedges and serve warm.

Heat spreadable fruit and water in small saucepan until warm; brush over fruit.

Nutritional Data

PER SERVING		EXCHANGES	
Calories:	244	Milk:	0.0
Fat (gm):	3.5	Veg.:	0.0
Cholesterol (mg):	0	Fruit:	1.5
Sodium (mg):	79	Bread:	1.5
Sat. fat (gm):	.6	Meat:	0.0
% Calories from fat:	14	Fat:	0.5

CASSATA SICILIANA

Filled with ricotta cheese, candied fruit, and chocolate chips, Cassata is an Italian dessert traditionally served during the Christmas holidays.

10 Servings

1 pkg. (6.95 ozs.) angel food loaf cake mix
½ cup water
1 cup low-fat ricotta cheese
¼ cup sugar
2 tablespoons mixed candied fruit, finely chopped
1 oz. semisweet chocolate, finely chopped
1 teaspoon lemon rind, grated
¼ cup dark rum
Chocolate Sauce (recipe follows)

P reheat oven to 375°.

Combine cake mix and water in large bowl. Mix at low speed until moistened. Beat 2 minutes at high speed. Pour into ungreased 9×5-inch loaf pan. Bake 25 to 30 minutes or until cracks on top appear dry. Cool completely in pan tipped on side on wire rack.

With a serrated knife, slice cake horizontally into three equal layers.

Combine ricotta cheese, sugar, candied fruit, chocolate, and lemon rind in small bowl.

Place 1 cake layer, crust side down, in a 9×5-inch loaf pan lined with plastic wrap. Brush cake with 1 tablespoon rum; spread with half of the ricotta mixture. Top with second cake layer, brush with 1 tablespoon rum, and spread with remaining ricotta mixture. Top with remaining cake layer, and brush with remaining rum. Cover with plastic wrap, pressing firmly to compact layers.

Refrigerate, weighted with a 16-ounce can, overnight. Slice cake and arrange on serving plate; drizzle with Chocolate Sauce.

Chocolate Sauce

¼ cup unsweetened cocoa
2 tablespoons sugar
1 tablespoon cornstarch
⅓ cup dark corn syrup
¼ cup 2% milk
1 teaspoon margarine
2 teaspoons vanilla

Combine cocoa, sugar, and cornstarch in small saucepan. Stir in corn syrup and milk until smooth. Cook over medium heat until mixture boils and thickens, stirring constantly. Remove from heat; stir in margarine and vanilla. Cool.

Nutritional Data

PER SERVING		EXCHANGES	
Calories:	217	Milk:	0.0
Fat (gm):	1.6	Veg.:	0.0
Cholesterol (mg):	2	Fruit:	1.0
Sodium (mg):	251	Bread:	2.0
Sat. fat (gm):	0	Meat:	0.0
% Calories from fat:	7	Fat:	0.0

Herbed Custard Brûlée

Scented with herbs, the delicate custard is topped with a sprinkling of caramelized sugar.

---

6 Servings

- 3 cups skim milk
- 2 tablespoons minced fresh, or ½ teaspoon dried basil leaves
- 2 tablespoons minced fresh, or ½ teaspoon dried cilantro leaves
- 2 tablespoons minced fresh, or ½ teaspoon dried tarragon leaves
- 5 eggs
- ½ cup granulated sugar
- 3 tablespoons packed light brown sugar

Preheat oven to 350°.

Combine milk, basil, cilantro, and tarragon in medium-size saucepan. Heat to boiling; remove from heat, cover, and let stand 10 minutes.

Meanwhile, beat eggs and granulated sugar in medium-size bowl 5 minutes or until pale yellow. Gradually add milk mixture to eggs, beating constantly.

Pour mixture into 8 custard cups or oven-proof ramekins. Place cups in 10×15-inch roasting pan; pour 2 inches hot water into pan. Bake 20 minutes or until knife inserted halfway between center and edge of custard comes out clean. Remove cups from roasting pan and cool to room temperature on wire rack. Refrigerate until completely chilled, 2 to 4 hours.

Preheat oven to 150°. Sprinkle brown sugar evenly in small baking dish and bake 10 minutes or until moisture is evaporated. (Do not melt sugar.)

Turn oven to broil. Sprinkle brown sugar evenly over chilled custards. Place on cookie sheet and broil, 4 inches from heat source, until sugar is melted and caramelized, 2 to 3 minutes. Serve immediately.

Nutritional Data

PER SERVING		EXCHANGES	
Calories:	192	Milk:	1.0
Fat (gm):	4.4	Veg.:	0.0
Cholesterol (mg):	180	Fruit:	0.0
Sodium (mg):	117	Bread:	1.0
Sat. fat (gm):	1.5	Meat:	0.0
% Calories from fat:	20	Fat:	1.0

*FRESH FRUIT WITH ROQUEFORT SHERBET

Fruit and cheese are popular dessert offerings. You'll enjoy the unique flavor and texture of this frosty cheese sherbet variation.

8 Servings

- 8 ozs. fat-free cream cheese, softened
- 1 oz. Roquefort or other blue-veined cheese
- ¼ cup sugar (substitute can be used*)
- ⅓ cup 2% milk
- ¼ cup lemon juice
- 2 pears, cored, sliced
- 2 apples, cored, sliced
- 1 pt. strawberries
- 8 small bunches seedless grapes (8 ozs.)

Beat cream cheese and Roquefort cheese in small bowl until smooth and fluffy. Beat in sugar,* milk, and lemon juice until smooth. Freeze in ice cream maker according to manufacturer's directions. Or pour mixture into 6×3-inch loaf pan, freeze until slushy, about 1 hour, then spoon into bowl and beat until fluffy; return to pan and freeze until firm, 6 hours or overnight.

To serve, scoop sherbet onto 4 plates; garnish with fruit.

Nutritional Data

PER SERVING			EXCHANGES		
Calories:	141	(121)	Milk:	0.0	
Fat (gm):	1.7		Veg.:	0.0	
Cholesterol (mg):	8		Fruit:	2.0	(1.5)
Sodium (mg):	226		Bread:	0.0	
Sat. fat (gm):	.8		Meat:	0.5	
% Calories from fat:	11	(12)	Fat:	0.0	

(*Changes shown in parentheses will result from substituting 6 packets Equal® for sugar.)

*CHOCOLATE YOGURT CHEESE WITH FRESH FRUIT

You won't believe that this richly flavored textured cheese is actually "skinny," with only 100 calories and 0 fat in a 2-ounce serving!

4 Servings

- 2 cups non-fat vanilla yogurt
- 2 tablespoons brown sugar (substitute can be used*)
- 2 teaspoons unsweetened cocoa
- 2 pears, sliced
- ½ pt. strawberries

Line a strainer with cheesecloth or a coffee filter and place over bowl. Spoon yogurt into lined strainer; cover with plastic wrap. Refrigerate 12 hours or until yogurt is reduced to 1 cup in volume and is the consistency of softened cream cheese; discard liquid.

Transfer yogurt cheese to small bowl, and stir in brown sugar* and cocoa until smooth. Refrigerate 1 to 2 hours for flavors to blend. Serve with fruit.

Nutritional Data

PER SERVING			EXCHANGES	
Calories:	169	(147)	Milk:	1.0
Fat (gm):	.6		Veg.:	0.0
Cholesterol (mg):	2		Fruit:	1.5 (1.0)
Sodium (mg):	56	(54)	Bread:	0.0
Sat. fat (gm):	0		Meat:	0.0
% Calories from fat:	3		Fat:	0.0

(*Changes shown in parentheses will result from substituting 3 packets Equal® for brown sugar.)

MINTED GOAT'S CHEESE WITH BLUEBERRIES

A Banon or Montrachet goat's cheese would be excellent. If preferred, low-fat or non-fat cream cheese can be substituted for the goat's cheese.

4 Servings

- 4 ozs. mild goat's cheese
- 1 tablespoon mint leaves, finely chopped
- ½ pt. blueberries
- 4 pcs. luncheon-size lavosh (5 inch)

Mix cheese and mint in small bowl until smooth; refrigerate 3 to 4 hours for flavors to blend. Shape cheese into flattened round on small, ovenproof serving plate.

Heat oven to 300°. Bake cheese until warm and slightly softened, 5 to 10 minutes.

Process ½ cup blueberries in food processor or blender until smooth. Spoon puree around cheese; sprinkle remaining blueberries over and around cheese. Serve with lavosh.

Nutritional Data

PER SERVING		EXCHANGES	
Calories:	145	Milk:	0.0
Fat (gm):	4.6	Veg.:	0.0
Cholesterol (mg):	13	Fruit:	1.0
Sodium (mg):	147	Bread:	0.0
Sat. fat (gm):	3	Meat:	1.5
% Calories from fat:	28	Fat:	0.0

FRESH GINGER SAUCE

Enjoy the intense sweet-hot flavor of fresh ginger root—wonderful over low-fat frozen vanilla yogurt, fresh fruit, or toasted angel food cake slices.

8 Servings (2 tablespoons each)

- 1 cup boiling water
- 2 tablespoons fresh ginger root, minced
- 3 tablespoons honey
- 2 tablespoons margarine
- 2 teaspoons lemon juice

Pour boiling water over ginger root and honey in small saucepan. Cover; let stand 30 minutes. Cook over medium heat until boiling; reduce heat and simmer 2 minutes. Remove from heat; stir in margarine and lemon juice. Serve warm or cold.

Nutritional Data

PER SERVING		EXCHANGES	
Calories:	40	Milk:	0.0
Fat (gm):	1.4	Veg.:	0.0
Cholesterol (mg):	0	Fruit:	0.0
Sodium (mg):	32	Bread:	0.0
Sat. fat (gm):	.2	Meat:	0.0
% Calories from fat:	32	Fat:	0.0

*CRÈME ANGLAISE

A thin, richly flavored French custard sauce that perfectly complements fresh fruit compotes and pies.

8 Servings (2 tablespoons each)

1 tablespoon cornstarch
2 teaspoons sugar (substitute can be used*)
1 cup skim milk
1 egg yolk
⅛-¼ teaspoon ground nutmeg

Mix cornstarch and sugar* in small saucepan; stir in milk. Cook over medium heat until mixture boils and thickens, stirring constantly.

Stir about ½ cup milk mixture into egg yolk; stir egg yolk mixture back into saucepan.

Cook over low heat, stirring constantly, until thickened. (Mixture will coat back of spoon.) Remove from heat; stir in nutmeg. Serve warm or cold.

*Note: If using sweeteners with aspartame, stir into sauce after it has been cooked and cooled.

Nutritional Data

PER SERVING			EXCHANGES	
Calories:	26	(22)	Milk:	0.0
Fat (gm):	.7		Veg.:	0.0
Cholesterol (mg):	27		Fruit:	0.5
Sodium (mg):	17		Bread:	0.0
Sat. fat (gm):	.2		Meat:	0.0
% Calories from fat:	24	(28)	Fat:	0.0

(*Changes shown in parentheses will result from substituting 1 packet Equal® for sugar.)

INDEX

A

Angel Food Cake, 15,16
Anise-Almond Biscotti, 61
Apple-Cranberry Crisp, 73
Apple Slices, 69
Apricot-Sesame Biscotti, 62

B

Baked Banana Souffle, 103
Baked Fruit Compotes in Parchment, 120
Baked Fruit Compote with Meringue Puffs, 76
Banana Cinnamon Cake, 5
Banana-Strawberry Cream Pie, 30
Bananas Foster, 70
Basic Pie Crust (All-Purpose Flour), 22
Basic Pie Crust (Cake Flour), 23
Berries 'n Cream Sauce, 115
Biscotti, 61, 62
Blueberry Bread Pudding, 92
Brandied Cherry Sauce, 109
Bread Pudding, 92
Brown Sugar Apple Pudding, 94
Brown Sugar Syrup, 94
Buñuelos with Fruit Salsa, 118

C

CAKES, 1–19
  Angel Food Cake with Orange Sauce, 15
  Banana Cinnamon Cake, 5
  Cassata Siciliana, 123

  Chocolate Buttermilk Layer Cake with Raspberry Cocoa Frosting, 10
  Chocolate Cherry Pudding Cake, 7
  Coffee-Frosted Cocoa Cake, 8
  Mocha Angel Food Cake with Bittersweet Chocolate Sauce, 16
  Orange Poppy Seed Cake, 14
  Pineapple-Lemon Trifle, 18
  Pumpkin Ginger Cake, 4
  Raspberry-Orange Swirl Cake, 17
  Rich Lemon Pound Cake, 12
  Streusel-Topped Carrot Cake, 2
Caramel-Apple Slices, 69
Caramel Flan, 99
Cardamom Crisps, 51
Carrot Cake, 2
Cassata Siciliana, 123
CHEESE
  Chocolate Yogurt Cheese with Fresh Fruit, 127
  Minted Goat's Cheese with Blueberries, 128
CHEESECAKES, 39–43
  Chocolate Fillo Cheesecake, 43
  Lemon Meringue Cheesecake, 42
  New York-Style Cheesecake, 41
  Spring Berry Cheesecake, 40
Cherry-Berry Grunt, 74
Chewy Cocoa Brownies, 53
Chilled Raspberry Souffle, 101
Chocolate Baked Alaska, 87
Chocolate Buttermilk Layer Cake with Raspberry Cocoa Frosting, 10
Chocolate Cherry Pudding Cake, 7
Chocolate Crinkles, 47
Chocolate Fillo Cheesecake, 43
Chocolate Fudge Meringues, 57
Chocolate Glaze, 52
Chocolate Glazed Cookie Crisps, 52
Chocolate Pudding, 90
Chocolate Rum Pie, 32
Chocolate Sauce, 114, 124
Chocolate Yogurt Cheese with Fresh Fruit, 127

Cinnamon Oatmeal Cookies, 48
Coffee-Frosted Cocoa Cake, 8
Coffee Frosting, 8
COOKIES, 45–62
  Anise-Almond Biscotti, 61
  Apricot-Sesame Biscotti, 62
  Cardamom Crisps, 51
  Chewy Cocoa Brownies, 53
  Chocolate Crinkles, 47
  Chocolate Fudge Meringues, 57
  Chocolate Glazed Cookie Crisps, 52
  Cinnamon Oatmeal Cookies, 48
  Favorite Sugar Cookies, 49
  Fig and Pear Bars, 55
  Gingersnappers, 46
  Glazed Chocolate Shortbread
    Squares, 50
  Hazelnut Macaroons, 60
  Orange-Almond Meringues, 58
  Peppermint Clouds, 59
  Sugared Lemon Squares, 54
Crème Anglaise, 130
Coulis, Raspberry, 106
CUSTARD, 89–103
  Caramel Flan, 99
  Fresh Apricot Custard, 98
  Herbed Custard Brûlée, 125
  Lemon Custard, 18
  Orange Flan, 100
  Peach Almond Cream, 97

Favorite Sugar Cookies, 49
Festive Cranberry Sauce, 110
Fig and Pear Bars, 55
Flan, 99, 100
Fresh Apricot Custard, 98
Fresh Berry Rhubarb, 67
FRESH FRUIT DESSERTS, 63-78
  Apple-Cranberry Crisp, 73
  Baked Fruit Compote with
    Meringue Puffs, 76
  Bananas Foster, 70
  Caramel Apple Slices, 69
  Cherry-Berry Grunt, 74
  Fresh Berry Rhubarb, 67
  Honey-Broiled Pineapple Slices, 66
  Honey-Lime Melon Wedges, 65
  Mixed Fruit Kabobs with
    Raspberry Sauce, 71
  Pears Belle Hélène, 75
  Spiced Orange Compote, 64
  Strawberry-Kiwi Shortcake, 72

  Sweet Cherry Soup with Yogurt
    Swirl, 78
  Tropical Fruit Soup, 77
  Wine Poached Plums, 68
Fresh Fruit with Roquefort Sherbet,
  126
Fresh Ginger Sauce, 129
FROSTINGS, GLAZES
  Chocolate Glaze, 52
  Coffee Frosting, 8
  Orange Glaze, 14
  Powdered Sugar Frosting, 5
  Raspberry Cocoa Frosting, 10
  Sugar Glaze, 50
  Vanilla Glaze, 51
FROZEN DESSERTS, 79–88
  Chocolate Baked Alaska, 87
  Frozen Peppermint Cake Rolls, 88
  Ginger-Citrus Sorbet, 81
  Lemon Ice, 82
  Mixed Fruit Tortoni, 85
  Orange Baked Alaska, 86
  Orange-Pineapple Sherbet, 80
  Pineapple-Champagne Ice, 85
  Praline Sundaes, 84
  Frozen Peppermint Cake Rolls, 88

Ginger-Citrus Sorbet, 81
Gingersnap Crumb Crust, 27
Gingersnappers, 46
Glazed Chocolate Shortbread
  Squares, 50
Graham Cracker Crumb Crust, 25

Hazelnut Macaroons, 60
Herb-Scented Citrus Cream, 116
Herbed Custard Brûlée, 125
Honey Sauce, 112
Honey-Broiled Pineapple Slices, 66
Honey-Lime Melon Wedges, 65

Indian Pudding, 93
Key Lime Pie, 33
Kiwi Tart, 34

L

Lemon Cloud Pie, 35
Lemon Custard, 18
Lemon Ice, 82
Lemon Meringue Cheesecake, 42
Lemon Syrup, 12
Lemon Velvet Pudding, 96

M,N

Macaroons, 60
Meringue Pie Crust, 24
Minted Goat's Cheese with
    Blueberries, 128
Mixed Fruit Kabobs with Raspberry
    Sauce, 71
Mixed Fruit Tortoni, 85
Mocha Angel Food Cake with
    Bittersweet Chocolate Sauce, 16
New York-Style Cheesecake, 41

O

Oatmeal Cookies, 48
Old-Fashioned Baked Rice Pudding,
    91
Old-Fashioned Buttermilk Pie, 28
Orange Baked Alaska, 86
Orange Flan, 100
Orange Glaze, 14
Orange Marmalade Sauce, 111
Orange-Almond Meringues, 58
Orange-Pineapple Sherbet, 80
Orange-Poppy Seed Cake, 14

P

Peach-Allspice Souffle, 102
Peach Almond Cream, 97
Pear Tart with Crème Anglaise, 38
Pears Belle Hélène, 75
Peppermint Clouds, 59
PIE CRUSTS
    Basic Pie Crust (All-Purpose
        Flour), 22
    Basic Pie Crust (Cake Flour), 23

Gingersnap Crumb Crust, 27
Graham Cracker Crumb Crust, 25
Meringue Pie Crust, 24
Vanilla Crumb Crust, 26
PIES AND TARTS, 21–43
    Banana-Strawberry Cream Pie, 30
    Chocolate Rum Pie, 32
    Key Lime Pie, 33
    Kiwi Tart, 34
    Lemon Cloud Pie, 35
    Old-Fashioned Buttermilk Pie, 28
    Pear Tart with Crème Anglaise, 38
    Raspberry-Glazed Blueberry Tart,
        37
    Rustic Country Fruit Tart, 122
    Spiced Sweet Potato Pie, 29
    Tarte Tatin, 36
    Toasted Coconut Cream Tart, 31
Pineapple-Champagne Ice, 83
Pineapple Lemon Trifle, 18
Pineapple-Rum Sauce, 107
Poppy Seed Cake, 14
Powdered Sugar Frosting, 5
Praline Sundaes, 84
PUDDINGS, 89–103
    Blueberry Bread Pudding, 92
    Brown Sugar Apple Pudding, 94
    Lemon Velvet Pudding, 96
    Old-Fashioned Baked Rice
        Pudding, 91
    Rich Chocolate Pudding, 90
    Warm Indian Pudding, 93
Pumpkin Ginger Cake, 4

R

Raspberry Cocoa Frosting, 10
Raspberry-Glazed Blueberry Tart, 37
Raspberry Orange Swirl Cake, 17
Rice Pudding, 91
Rich Chocolate Pudding, 90
Rich Lemon Pound Cake, 12
Rum Sauce, 107, 113
Rustic Country Fruit Tart, 122

S

SAUCES, 105–116
    Berries 'n Cream Sauce, 115
    Bittersweet Chocolate Sauce, 114
    Brandied Cherry Sauce, 109
    Chocolate, 114, 124

Crème Anglaise, 130
Festive Cranberry Sauce, 110
Fresh Ginger Sauce, 129
Herb-Scented Citrus Cream, 116
Honey Sauce, 112
Orange Marmalade Sauce, 111
Pineapple-Rum Sauce, 107
Summer Raspberry Coulis, 106
Tart Lemon Sauce, 108
Warm Rum Sauce, 113
Shortbread, 50
Shortcake, 72
SOUFFLES, 89–103
Baked Banana Souffle, 103
Chilled Raspberry Souffle, 101
Peach-Allspice Souffle, 102
Soups, Fruit, 77, 78
Spiced Orange Compote, 64
Spiced Sweet Potato Pie, 29
Spring Berry Cheesecake, 40
Strawberries with Peppercorns, 119
Strawberry-Kiwi Shortcake, 72
Streusel-Topped Carrot Cake, 2
Sugar Cookies, 49, 54
Sugar Glaze, 30
Sugared Lemon Squares, 54
Summer Raspberry Coulis, 106

Sweet Cherry Soup with Yogurt
  Swirl, 78

Tart Lemon Sauce, 108
Tarte Tatin, 36
Toasted Coconut Cream Tart, 31
Tortoni, 85
Trifle, 18
Tropical Fruit Soup, 77

Vanilla Crumb Crust, 26
Vanilla Glaze, 51
Warm Indian Pudding, 93
Warm Rum Sauce, 113
Wine Poached Plums, 68

INSTRUCTOR'S RESOURCE GUIDE

Educating
Exceptional Children
Fourth Edition

CONTAINS:

- suggestions for easily incorporating Annual Editions into instructional programs
- summaries of each article
- over 100 multiple choice test questions
- hundreds of essay and discussion questions

Using EDUCATING EXCEPTIONAL CHILDREN, Fourth Edition in the Classroom
AN INSTRUCTOR'S RESOURCE GUIDE

This guide has been prepared for instructors using *Annual Editions: Educating Exceptional Children, Fourth Edition,* as required reading in their classrooms. It provides a wealth of summary, discussion, and testing material for the 52 articles contained in this volume. Taken together with the substantial amount of organizing features in this volume itself we hope it will make the use of Annual Editions easier and more enjoyable. Like Annual Editions this guide will be revised regularly. Therefore, any suggestions you have for improving it are welcome. We appreciate your use of Annual Editions in your classes.

Contents

Using Annual Editions for Teaching   3
The Annual Editions Instructor's Resource   5
   Guide—Design and Use
The Question Bank   8

Annual Editions
Copyright 1988 by The Dushkin Publishing Group, Inc.
Guilford, Connecticut 06437
ISBN: 0-87967-706-6
Printed in U.S.A.
Instructors using Annual Editions in the classroom have
the Dushkin Publishing Group's permission to duplicate
questions for classroom use.